Cabin Journal

by

Yvonne Pepin

Illustrated by the Author

SHAMELESS HUSSY PRESS

ISBN 0-915288-49-4

SHAMELESS HUSSY PRESS
P.O. Box 3092
Berkeley, CA 94703

TO MY PARENTS

Cabin Journal is a real account of my life at age 18 as I brazenly and oftentimes awkwardly set out to define my relationship to myself and others.

Now, 11 years later, I have transcribed 24 spiral notebooks, the actual journals, and compiled artwork from this past to complete *Cabin Journal.* I have changed the names of the people and places in this book in order to protect their privacy.

—Yvonne Pepin

I am the wild child of this mountainside
No one's daughter, I hide from intrusions
and dance alone in full moonlight, naked
and shimmering under white.

I follow few rules but those that rule
warm days, nights cool, sun and star
motion, the cyclical flows.

I am the wild child who choreographs trees
to winds and swims in creeks beside trout flicker.

I am a wild child fed on earth.

I have stalked with deer, set snare
for hunting men and sat the day in
hot summer humm, coyote paw patter.

I am a wild child and the mountain is stern
she has flung me like a young cone
to the earth before I was ready to
ease from her birth

but she is gentle her hills like breasts roll
give me shelter in and from myself.

A wild child I have walked alone
had no home and lived in fear.

I have kindled fires where there was cold
and learned my name.

I am a wild child flung to earth
I cling to the spiral of my birth.

✣ March 21, 1975

The piercing whistle. The teakettle calls, and I answer it by pouring its roiling liquid into my mug made of Red Wing pottery.

Outside, the blizzard is slamming snow gusts and rattling the windowpanes. The weathermen say this is the worst storm in Minnesota for a century, with winds from 60 to 100 miles per hour and snow accumulation up to 20 inches. But I don't want to talk about the weather that drives me inside the shelter of my little St. Paul apartment. I want to talk about what I'm doing now at the kitchen table: making lists. Lists of what to bring to Oregon: tools, food supplies, rugged clothes, first-aid kit, heavy boots, my drawing and painting things, and other implements that will allow me luxury in this new rural life style.

Along with the tea my mind steeps with ideas and things to pull together before we leave for Pine Valley, that tiny Oregon town that is to be our new home. I will leave the neon splash of the Twin Cities and venture west to build a new life in the mountains with a woman I am unsure of building with anymore.

The only thing I am certain of now, looking out the window at the graceful bend of the elm trees collecting snow in their boughs, is that I want to be an artist. I want to study the patterns of nature—bark and sand, the geometry of a flower, the form of the land—and convey the inlaid spirit of nature through my drawings and paintings.

✣ March 22

Today I am Virginia Woolf in Levis, hiking boots, and a plaid shirt. I scour the campus of this elite, all-female Catholic college in search of the library. I am Virginia Woolf only because I feel as if I have been banned from this campus of St. Catherine's, like Virginia was banned from Oxford. Even in "Sisterhood" there is discrimination. I am aware I don't fit the standards of the color-coordinated collegiates by the judgmental stares I draw.

To fit in here means that you have to have thousands of

dollars, or parents who have thousands of dollars, to pay the tuition required to study at St. Catherine's. I have neither, thousands or parents, and quit believing in God after my mother died. I just come here to use the library because it is close to my apartment and I like to savor the ambience of a community of intellectually inclined women.

I decide to rein my attempt of flushing out the library amid the carefully planned droppings of well-built brick architecture. I am tired of walking through the death of another Minnesota winter that absorbs into my pant cuffs hanging over and dragging behind my heels.

I lean against a slush-spackled bench and watch some nuns behind a big plate-glass window. From my vantage, I see them spoon prunes from a can into bowls, which when filled are passed clockwise around the table to waiting nuns. Under the

fluorescent lights in the dining hall, the women exude halos, and despite some myth, I do not think nuns in habit are comparable to the likes of penguins. Behind the sameness of the nuns' black and white exteriors lie individual spirits. I envy nuns; they live out a part of me that seeks reverence through silent communion with women and nature.

I sit and survey more of my surroundings—the collegiates who cascade over the campus between megaphoned strikes of the chapel bell. I watch them, fresh-faced images of the idealized young woman. They harbor their books to bosoms covered in expensive coats, and scurry like squirrels into hollow oaks of intellect to crack the shell of their cache.

I feel some jealousy and resentment towards these women, the way some will continue to represent our sex. I am envious because of the degree of ease many of these women have had in their lives and will continue to have as long as they bend to men in female submission. These women go from mommy and daddy to hubby, supporters who will continue to feather the nest and pad the fall after chanced flights. I am neither a part of this nor a resurrection off the fashion page.

I continue to observe the nuns spooning prunes from a can labeled "Stewed Prunes." I take an inside estimate of my life and wonder at its movement. I try to label myself like a can of prunes, but cannot come up with a title as distinct as the name on the can.

I am Yvonne. I am a woman. I am a bisexual? I am a lesbian? I am eighteen years old. My name, age, and sex are the only labels I can slap on my fine-boned container.

+ March 25

This is a journal, I conclude, after having been given the definitions of what constitutes a journal, a diary, a log. This journal is a result of fulfilling the assignment doled out by my Creative Writing instructor, Lyle Franklin.

Maybe my efforts won't be as worthy as Anaïs Nin's or Sylvia Plath's, but I've got the gump to give writing a try. But don't all writers carry around portable typewriters, have gaunt faces, and smoke cigarettes? How can I be a writer if I continue to carry a knapsack chock-full of pencils and a

sketch pad? Just sitting here now trying to formulate frag-
ments of my thoughts into some feasible order has caused me
to bite three of my fingernails to the skin. So maybe I will
never learn to write. What have I got to lose? Plenty, that's
what. Mainly patience and fingernails. That's enough to dis-
courage me.

This is my last week as a student at a community college,
where the tuition is more in accordance with my finances. I
started spring semester yesterday, but will attend only the
first two weeks of classes. My first class is Advanced Creative
Writing.

Lyle Franklin is a man in his middle forties, with long hair
that he keeps tied back in a tight ponytail. Keeping a journal
was his idea. I am afraid to turn it in or even to take it to him
for criticism because he will find out that I am a lesbian.
Funny how people change attitudes when they find out
you're "one of those."

✝ March 30

Jesus Christ and I are resurrected from the dead. It is
Easter morning, 3 A.M. I am sitting in the living room, listening to a string quartet on the stereo.

The day has been spent with Jean, both of us getting in
touch with the other. Jean is the disclosure in my life I am
hesitant to disclose, perhaps because of my staunch Catholic
upbringing, perhaps because of the ill effects that disclosing
one's homosexuality has on others.

Jean is the woman I have lived with for over two years. We
are lovers. And we love each other—though this statement
may seem in non-agreement once the state of our affair is
thoroughly disclosed.

Jean and I took time out today to reunite ourselves in a
loving way and did not get out of bed until after noon, a
rarity in the midst of our get-it-together-to-move-to-Oregon
act. In the afternoon we did mushrooms and went to Taylors Falls. We perched on the jets of gray granite rock looming above the rootbeer-colored St. Croix River. I started to
think about the changes our relationship has gone through
and how it will continue to change after we move to Oregon.

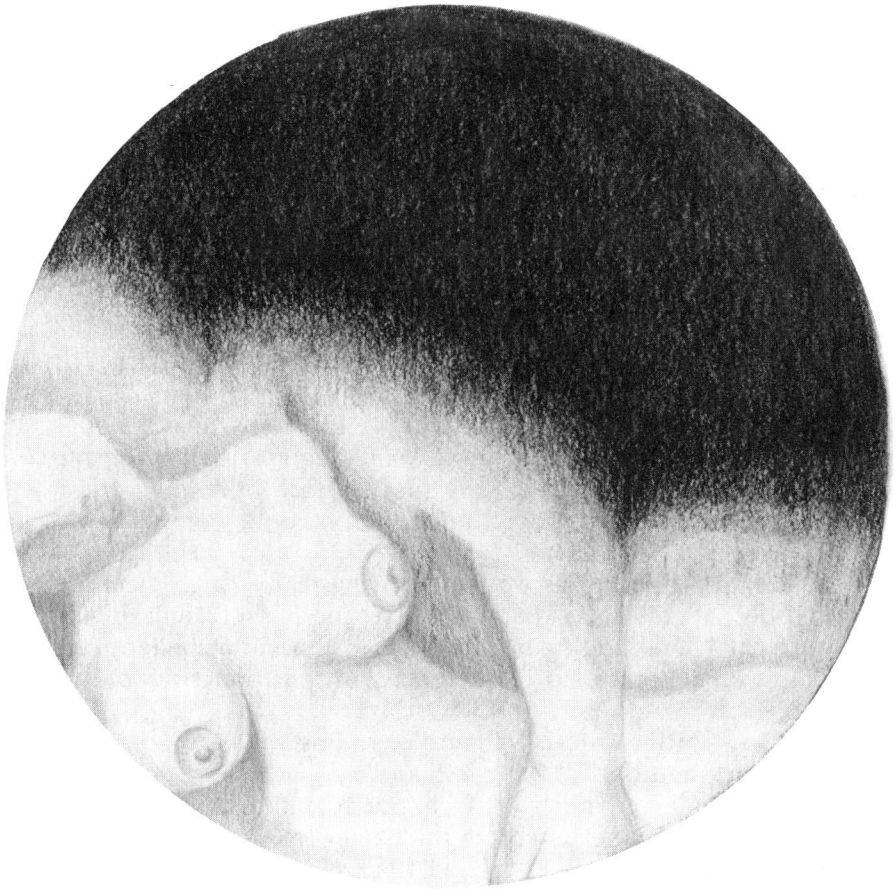

We talked about how we will leave in a few weeks to establish new lives in Oregon, to create our dream of building a log cabin and living together in the mountains. This dream, though, feels tainted by unresolved feelings between us that rub raw and leave us sore with each other.

I wonder about our capabilities. Will we be able to build a log cabin, knowing only that log cabins are built out of logs? Will Jean be able to make a clean emotional break from Tony?

Tony: He seems to be more of a barrier in getting to Oregon than the two thousand miles separating us from our vision of being two women contending with our lives in the wilds. Tony has captured a part of Jean's heart I won't feed, a part of her heart that is making the getaway to Oregon sticky business.

✛ March 31

Today Jean and I begin buying supplies for the trip west. At the co-op in Minneapolis we bought twenty-five pounds of wheat berries, corn, powdered milk, whole grain flour, and some dried fruit. On the way home we stopped at the Salvation Army and bought three beat-up trunks to pack our clothes in.

This evening I had dinner with Jay Ellen, my poet friend. I planned to tell her about my sexuality, about my relationship with Jean. This was to be my first big step in coming out. I was very apprehensive, felt my honesty would jeopardize our friendship.

I finally told her as we were getting ready to go meet her mother at Mickey's Bar. At first she didn't believe me, thought I was kidding her, like usual. But her disbelief probably came because of my nonchalant introduction of the subject.

"Oh, by the way, Jay Ellen," I said as we were going out the apartment door, "I'm a lesbian."

We didn't get much of a chance to talk about it on the short drive to the bar or at the bar in front of her mother. But later, when Jay Ellen and I left, she assured me underneath the neon drip of the bar sign outside on the sidewalk that it's okay with her; she thinks everyone is bisexual. She gave me a real hug good night.

I return home at 3:30 A.M. Jean and I have another argument. It's about things that I've stored up inside me, things that are hard for me to talk about. Like my inability to have sex with Jean or anyone right now and my jealousy and resentment of Tony—"Why do you need a man lover when you have me?"—and forty-two other things boiling beneath the surface of my skin.

Why can't I make love to this woman whom I have made my idol, my one-and-only, for two years? Always her needs come before meeting my own, and my pleasure is to please her. Now there is some undefined turn of my disposition towards her.

My love for her is still strong, or I wouldn't be going through all this conflict now. Ever since she began getting tight with Tony, I have felt myself turning inside myself and drawing away from Jean, closing down those avenues I used to let pulse with desire.

In the last few months of love-making, it has been difficult to respond to her touch. My mind won't let me experience the sensations of my body. I close down and think about Tony and Jean and am filled with dark and red emotions. Jean says that she feels more pleasure in making love to me than with Tony, but I can't buy it.

Tony, that's the reason, the source behind the force that has caused me to shut down to Jean's gestures of love.

✣ April 1, 1975

Wake up this morning, and Jean is trying to make love to me. I can't enjoy her touch, don't feel any pleasure, and pull my breast from her mouth. Her sobs are real—loud and wet. They join our bodies with warm moisture from her tears. My tears are on her cheeks, her tears are running down my forehead. We hold each other, saying "I love you" between sobs.

She says she has to go over to Tony's to work on the trailer we will be taking to Oregon, and she gets out of bed. I am curled tight into a ball, with tears running down my cheeks into the silken blue sheets on the waterbed. As she is ready to go she says, "I don't like to leave you like this," zips her parka, and walks out the door.

Haven't brushed my hair all day, and baggy clothes hang from my disenchanted frame. Four phone calls today.

Phone call #1: Dell wants to see me before we go to Oregon.

Phone call #2: Susan, who bought a drawing of mine from the show I had at Metro, tells me she wants to return it because she is not comfortable with it anymore. She says it is excellent, but it leaves her feeling cold and her apartment is so small that she wants only warm things in it. She is still

7

willing to pay for the drawing, but she wants to give it back. I say no to this offer because then she would be paying me to just look at the drawing for a while. We decide I will keep ten dollars and the drawing. I'm sorry she's returning it, but happy that it can pull such strong feelings from someone. At eighteen my art is becoming known and rejected!

Phone call #3: June Harting, my lawyer, my princess in shining armor, my own pursuer of justice, has returned my call. The mysterious siphoning of my dead parents' trust fund is beginning to clarify. When she hears the new developments in the story, June calls my relatives "bastards." I agree. She says to stay calm, she will call me on Monday, and Happy Easter.

One last phone call, #4: Jean. She will not be home for supper. "Is that all right?" "Yeah," I say. "Are you all right?" "Yeah," I say and hang up.

✝ April 3

Jumbled, in ultimate chaos, I sit rocking in this chair like a Vietnamese woman who surveys her bombed-out village. The apartment is a disaster area of packed and unpacked objects of our very material life style.

This has been a day of moving, separating, boxing, packing and unpacking for the move from this St. Paul apartment to a tree-and-snow-covered Oregon mountainside. The lifting of many boxes has made me painfully aware of every muscle that was pulled from hibernation.

The days until leaving for Pine Valley are a minimal number, and those days, full and hard with preparations to complete. I will miss my possessions—dishes, dolls, candles, grandfather clock, tapestries rich and colorful, paintings and prints in frames, oak and solid.

✝ April 4

Back to the fast pace through the slush of the city streets. I woke at 5:30 A.M. and washed my hair before catching the 7:01 A.M. Selby-Lake Street bus that would deliver me to an 8 A.M. watercolor class at Metro.

I went back to bed after I bathed, and asked Jean if she would take me to school when she went over to Tony's to work on the trailer. The fumes from riding the bus in the morning make me sick. Jean said yes, and I crawled back beside her.

We had another argument last night, and nothing this morning was resolved. The argument was about our all-time butt-heads-and-break-hearts-over topic, Tony. To state it bluntly, I am jealous. Before Tony and Jean became lovers, he and I were good friends. Now there is only anger and bitterness towards each other.

I lie down on top of Jean. My body is cold, hers is still warm with sleep. My chill evaporates in her warmth. I think of how mean and nasty I can get sometimes and wonder why anybody wants to have a relationship with me. If Jean put me through the tests I have put her through and slighted me the way I have her, I think I would have up and left long ago. But she continues to put up with my ornery disposition, knowing by now it won't last long.

I hate myself when this ugly Yvonne comes out. Other people hate this ugly Yvonne, too. I wonder if all people have uglies inside themselves.

Jean is glad I am not angry with her anymore. She kisses my neck and eyes softly. "I love you," she says. I burrow my face into her neck and repeat the cliché. She smells sweet and sleepy, and we lie together in a semiconscious phase; my wet hair, in cold seaweed strands, tangles between us.

A little sleep snort comes from Jean, which opens both our eyes, and we grin and hold each other tighter. I am warm now, warm from Jean. Our bodies, so much alike in structure and size, fit together like liquid. Every curve is met with a curve.

When we sleep, we hold each other, like elbow macaroni. There are nights when, because of some difference, she is on one side of the king-sized waterbed, and I, on the opposite side trying to sleep, feel empty, as if something has drained us of the love we have for each other. On these nights I curl around my pillow, the way Jean would hold me.

I make love to Jean. Annabelle the cat is in her usual position, hovering right over us, looking on like a vulture surveying carrion. Perhaps her feline instincts detect the decay between us that neither Jean nor I have the courage to confront. We are softened by an attempt of sun through this gray Minnesota day.

✛ April 5

Run to Tony; he will comfort you when I cannot. He will comfort you when I will not.

I wander the city this day. Sunshine, 30 above zero, an early spring day. This morning I install the tape deck in Jean's jeep. My hands get numb. I drop the Phillips screwdriver. Reaching for it I find on the jeep floor a folded piece of paper. I know it's from Tony to Jean. I should not unfold it, but I can't stop.

I bleed to death, reading a poem from Tony about making love to Jean. Instant abortion. All feeling inside me scraped clean by these loving words that trespass on my territory. Tony loves Jean. Yvonne loves Jean. A triangle. I am the ragged end, the scrap, the leftover.

I am supposed to console that part of Jean that Tony cannot. I am hurt, knowing this. I will hurt even more getting out of it. In a few days I will be leaving to live twenty-four hours a day with a woman I love, a woman I do not want to love.

My need now is to be me. To learn to hold myself when I cry. To comfort myself when I hurt. To be free of this addiction to love. To be defined by myself, not by someone else. In living with this woman for two years I have become just part of a "we," not a "me." I have become Yvonne and Jean. I just want to be Yvonne.

✛ April 8

Tonight, sitting in the pine chair, the cat on my lap, I drink Zeller Jelzwarze Katz German wine in confusion. My immediate relationships are scrambled, jumbled, incomprehensible. My sexuality undetermined. My written mode of expression trite.

It is late. I have to rise two and a half hours before the sun tomorrow, and even though I don't feel like sleeping, I will go to bed, knowing that sleep will help subdue pain and confusion.

I go to bed at 12:45 A.M., but get up at 2:45 A.M. I cannot sleep due to coffee and anxiety. I lay in bed for that hour and a half waiting for the rumble of the jeep, the final rev of the engine, the sound of its door being slammed closed, the key turning admittance into the security door, and finally the last key inside the lock to our apartment. I think anxiety will subside when Jean is in the apartment. When she is in bed, I will tell her I don't want a sexual relationship with her anymore.

The sounds she makes preparing for bed annoy me. I put the pillows over my head, hoping for sleep to pass over me soon, before she comes to bed. I try to think of things to pull me into the cave of slumber and remember the cheddar cheese left in my knapsack from the fondue supper Jay Ellen and I had earlier this evening. I get out of bed to put it in the refrigerator. Jean is in the bathroom. She says, "Hi." I throw the cheese in the already cluttered refrigerator and make my way back to the bedroom without responding to Jean.

On the table in the living room are a dozen pink roses Jean has just brought home and arranged in the tall black Playboy mug we use as a vase. They are a gift from Tony. The blade in my heart edges in deeper. The blood I bleed now is darker. I have bled so much today that if I bleed tomorrow, the painful liquid will be black.

Back in bed. The pillow is over my head. I do not realize until minutes later that my fists are clenched into balls. I keep trying to tell myself to relax, that this is all in my head. When she comes to bed, I feel her crawl over me and lie far on the opposite side. I am relieved she has not tried to touch me. I am angry at not having the chance to tell her not to touch me.

We are both awake, wide awake, my eyes like glaring plates beneath covers of closed lids. We are both cold marble tombstones, relaying the death of our relationship—only "to rest in peace" will not come tonight.

✛ April 9

I'm beginning to see my position with people close to me, how hard I am to understand, temperamental. I'm hard. I am trying to make a more independent, understanding me.

Friday night Jean and I had verbal warfare. She left and did not come back that night. I cried a lot, was hurt, slept in a bed meant for two, lost, detached. I woke frequently and eyed the clock, wondering when Jean was coming home, knowing she wouldn't.

In the morning, waking to an empty apartment felt like there had been a death inside the night before. Knowing that staying in the apartment alone would allow me opportunity to hurt myself more, I left for my sister's house. I am here now, sleeping in a bag in the small, cold living room. It is after 3 A.M. Two dogs sleeping next to me have nightmares on the floor.

✛ April 17

Drive under gray South Dakota sky, behind mud-spackled windshield, past naked fields, patches of dying snow, black and white magpies, and towns with names of Murdo, Kadoka, Cottonwood, and Wall, the town raped by advertising signs. I have been on the road for twenty hours. Already sights and feelings have been plentiful.

Last night on the drive through South Dakota, a hailstorm caused us to pull to the side of endless Highway 90 to wait it out. The sound of bouncing hail on the metal roof was frightening. We curled in the back and slept for three hours.

Back on the road I drive through thick fog, only able to travel at 20 mph and even then have difficulty seeing the highway lines. Towards 8:00 A.M., I become very tired and stop at a truck stop to shock myself awake with water. I walk into the cafe, tuck in my plaid shirt, and give a yank on my jeans.

The truckers eating their breakfast look at me and point and smile. I am a trucker with long brown hair and a small turquoise ring on my finger. I am proud to be among these machine-driving men. I pay the waitress 26 cents for a small styrafoam cup of hot brown speed, take two toothpicks from the counter, put them in my breast pocket, yank my jeans on my hip again, and nod back to the truckers. One trucker calls me pint sized.

Back on the road, my coffee cup empty, I place one of the toothpicks in my mouth and chew and spin it around as I have seen the men in the cafe do. Bouncing on the black leather seat and straining to see over the steering wheel, I want to paint a portrait of this pint-sized trucker complete with toothpick.

In Gillette, Wyoming, I walk into another truck stop, not for coffee like the other truckers, but to acquire a bag to hold my roasted soybeans. I'll wager I'm the only trucker in this truck stop today who has to change a tampax.

✛ April 18

I sit on the sidewalk in Worland, Wyoming, writing in front of the IGA store, and draw stares from the townspeople. It is a sunny 55, birds are singing, mountains surround me on two sides, and I am happy to be alive and feel warm rays shining on my hair and face.

Yesterday proved to be an event-filled day. Our drive through the Big Horn was very scenic, despite blowing snow and steep curved roads clothed in ice. Jean was driving through Powder River and did not see the two boulders in the road. She swerved around the smaller one, but we were headed for the big boulder. She slammed on the brakes. The trailer jack-knifed, and we gave each other looks of stone fright as we headed for a plunge into the rocky gorge below. I was ready to jump from the jeep, but decided to take the bloody dive with Jean.

Looking out the window, seeing the bottom, feeling the trailer pull us over, I braced myself for the last few minutes of my life. The jeep jerked to a stop. We looked at each other. I leaned over and put my head on Jean's shoulder for a second and said, "Fuck, we're alive."

We got out of the jeep quickly, thinking we could still be pulled over by the weight of the trailer hanging over the bank. When I jumped out in my stocking feet, I saw that the trailer had broken off the hitch and crashed down the mountain slope. All our planning, packing, and saving lay at the top, middle, and bottom of a red rocky cliff on the Powder River Pass. The snow would cover up our belongings faster than we could recognize them.

Sliding down among the debris, I saw my 25-pound container of soybeans broken and aborted of all its protein-packed pellets. All the planning I put into making sure we would get proper protein through the combination of different legumes was now combined with the snow and rock of the Big Horn Mountains. I felt like a pioneer woman crossing Donner Pass, looking down, discouraged, after just having my covered wagon crash over a cliffside, taking with it all my possessions needed to carve a new life in the wilderness.

Neither Jean nor I said much, but we just started to haul up what we could salvage. But what had first priority? The food? The tools? Trunks? I decided my art supplies first. At the point of discouragement when I was ready to leave everything to this cliffside in this snowstorm, two men stopped their trucks to help with rescue operations. One of the men, Jake, said we could put what wouldn't fit in our jeep into his truck and repack at his garage in Worland, a town about 30 miles from the wreck.

We drive on, wet and shivering with chill to the bone from wonderful Wyoming's snow. Joni Mitchell plays "Lady of the Canyon" on the tape deck. I snicker at the irony, thankful I am not a lady of the canyon. Another eight inches of the jeep's rear tire and I would have been pulp at the canyon bottom along with everything else mangled in the tumble. I am so thankful for my life I want to scream it. For the first time in my life, I really value my life, living.

We meet Jake at the Washakie Grill in Worland. He buys us coffee and tells everyone of our experience. The customers and waitress are amazed that we are sitting there drinking coffee and telling of our adventure. We learn Powder River Pass is notorious for taking lives and that Jean and I are the first people Worland has seen walk away from it after a wreck.

I spend three hours repacking the jeep. I have had five hours of sleep in the last three days and am now overcome with fatigue and muscle soreness from the jolt of the accident, hauling everything up the cliff, and lifting the trunks on top of the jeep. We spend the night at Jake's house. I feel at home in this warm house and fall asleep minutes after getting in bed, with Jean holding me very tightly.

✝ April 19

Meridian, Idaho. I sit in Pat's Cafe, drinking coffee with the truckers. Two hundred fifty miles and we will be in Pine Valley. I write in my journal, and the other truckers eye me. Again I am the only trucker in this stop-over with a menstrual flow.

Afternoon: Green grass over the border. We are in Oregon. We stop at a rest area. We both dance and leap on the soft grass, alien to our winter-conditioned feet. In the descent of a leap, I am received by Jean's outstretched arms. Our chests thud together. We dance and kiss at the rest area in Ontario, Oregon.

✝ April 20

I wake to winter-shedding sounds of swollen running creeks. Crisp morning air is scented with ponderosa pine, and the sky is clear. Arrived at my brother's camp yesterday and spent the night.

Mark is a future blacksmith. Last year he was being a moto cross biker, the year before that a hobbit. Now he has found an identity with this land he owns twenty-five miles, as the crow flies, from my land. Brad, Mark's friend, is staying with him to help build Mark a log cabin. Brad is

twenty-four, big and hearty as his heart. His cherry nose and cheeks pop from the soft brown hair on his face.

Driving to Mark's yesterday, we stopped to see some neighbors of his, Chris and Dale, mother and father of three-year-old Sophie and six-month-old Jud. They have lived in these mountains outside of Pine Valley not even a year, in a small cabin Dale built in a setting of ponderosa pine. They have goats, a barn, an underground refrigerator, and a lot of love. Dale mentioned he was looking for work. I offered him a job helping me build, and he said he would work for two dollars an hour because that is how much he was paid for hauling milk in Idaho. Chris is sensitive, a woman with hair black and soft, like Mogus, their cat. Sophie, their daughter, is small and full of energy like a spring day. Jud is still a baby boy and drools when he smiles.

✛ April 21

After leaving Mark's camp we stopped in town to visit Fred Simpson and his wife, Josie, who own 160 acres below me. Made arrangements to stay in an old cabin on his land until the snow melts enough on my 80 so we can live up there in a tent. I sensed Fred was trying to protect me as if I were his young daughter. I also got this feeling from Jake.

The roads up to my land are still under two feet of snow. We parked the jeep in the Doctor's meadow below my land and had to pack our things over the hillsides. Halfway across the meadow, a burly man in baggy jeans held up by suspenders stopped his chain saw, left it near the tree he was buzzing up, and came over to see who the intruders were. The Doc is my closest neighbor when he is at his cabin on weekends. His cheeks rose higher with a little grin when we told him that we are his new neighbors and are going to build a cabin up on my property.

Our packs are heavy with two days' worth of provisions, pots, and books. I had to carry Annabelle the two snowy miles because she wouldn't walk on her leash.

The cabin is a disappointment in luxury, something Snuffy Smith would turn his nose up at. It is about eighty years old, a 14' x 18' stockade-style log cabin, with a leaky roof, cracks

between the floorboards, and walls which are packed with scampering mice, there is a nice wood-burning cookstove inside and some ratted furniture. The creek runs right outside the door, so water is close at hand.

Jean and I got a fire going in the stove by pouring lantern fuel on the wet kindling. The lantern is broken, so all the illumination we have is from one tiny candle and what light pours out from the little opened door on the firebox. The cabin has not gotten any warmer than the temperature outside, which tonight is so cold I can write only for a few minutes before needing to thaw my fingers on the stovetop. I don't know what is colder tonight, the spring thaw or the freeze-up in communication between Jean and me.

✝ April 22

This land of towering pine tree silhouettes, of rich, deep forested interiors, and whispering creeks is like a déjà vu—I have been here before. Then, it was only a place I could touch with my inner vision and not reach out and feel as I can now through the sensation of branches crossing my face while I tear through my new home with the eagerness of a six-year-old child.

I squat on my haunches and rock back and forth on the balls of my thick boots. I watch the white water dance over boulders in the swelling creek. I survey the situation of my life. I have made it! Made it to this land I once only dreamed of, made it into the home I sorely needed after the ping-pong existence of being an orphan, a ward of the state, a foster child.

I made this land my reality last year after venturing, fresh from high school graduation in Minnesota, to comb the west for land. It's a lucky fact that this Oregon mountainside claimed me after all the realtors told me I would never find what I wanted—a secluded place of virgin forest in the mountains with a stream running year round. The realtors told me everyone was looking for the same utopia, only that type of land had been bought up and logged fifty years ago. Instead, they showed me sagebrush and juniper land, infested with rattlesnakes, that sold for two thousand dollars an acre. But I persisted, as is my nature, and followed my intuition, good fortune, and business sense to find, then buy this property with my inheritance.

This land loomed into my vision the night my mother died. "It was God's will," the priest piously informed me. I turned from him and the expectant faces of my relatives, inside myself. My mother was dead, and I did not want the condolences of well-meaning but pretentiously sentimental, juicy-eyed

aunts. Suddenly I was something that happened only to other people: an orphan.

"Orphan." The word seeped messages into my bones of a haunted house full of mystery. I could imagine it, having stood beneath dark shuttered windows, looking upwards at something I had yet to experience. Death pulled me from my vantage into the darkened interior, where I was made to find insight to direct me through dark passages untouched by light.

Curled into myself that night on a cot in somebody else's basement, I knew then that as soon as I became of age and was out from under the ruling hand of a legal guardian, trust officer, and probate judge, I was going to take my money and buy land. I saw the land clearly that night. My vision was of a dark wooded hollow with a log cabin. I was going to live there alone with a cat and write poetry . . .

I am living my vision now. Some of the circumstances have changed, but I have found this land and with it my home. I made it through the maze and know that it takes toughness and persistence to build the strength to get what I want.

✛ April 23

Cripes! Here it is almost May, and the snow on the road leading up to my land crests near my knees with every step I take.

I walked around my land today, surveying potential building sites. Some places on the north slope had snow piled as high as my crotch. It's hard to move through this stuff. It's not the type of powder I've skied on at Alta, but heavy snow that impedes the body's movements.

Tonight when the sun began to go down, I decided it was time to return to the old cabin. I was soaked and cold from my rendezvous and ran back down the mountain in hopes that Jean would help me warm up. Tonight we will have to discuss our relationship—what there is left of it.

✛ April 24

The weather today, like my energy, has fluctuated from clear to cloudy. Last night I seduced the brandy bottle into emptiness with my greedy lips.

20

I had it out with Jean last night, yelled and screamed and cried about all I've stored up over the past months. We were outside by a campfire, and in my display of emotions I became oblivious to the flames and burned my pantleg, boot laces, and socks drying on a rock. I've come to the conclusion alcohol and the mountains don't make it easy together.

This morning I woke up with a hangover and stuck my head in the liquid ice waters of the creek in anticipation of reviving my corpse.

In the afternoon I took up axe and saw and walked to the top of my land to cut tipi poles with Jean. We sweated on the walk up and took off our shirts. My skin was the color of a deer against the dying white snow. We embraced after crossing the fence to my land. Our nipples against each other's skin were hard from the mountain's chill. I told Jean, "Your nipples remind me of raspberries."

After our clearing out of pent-up emotions last night, we seem to be feeling a more honest communication. We seem to know where each stands in relation to the other, and it is not with the same footing we once used to hoist up our love. Our relationship has changed because of steps we needed to take in our individual growth. Jean has decided to do more stepping in the direction of Tony. Out of necessity I will have to learn to walk more with myself. This is clear—our relationship has changed, and the degree to which we exhibit our love daily. This is going to be hard to stick to, the fact that I can't hang on to what won't be there for me anymore.

✛ April 25

The gray spiral of smoke signaled me over the mountain to Jean and a pot of soup cooking on the stove. The day has been long, and I am learning to use daylight to full capacity by writing out of doors before the sun sets.

Met Dale in town today to discuss building plans and work terms. I bought my first log cabin building tool at the hardware store, a metal-handled hatchet. Dale came up to my land with me. We sat on the building location I had selected, and he drew diagrams of cabin constructions in the snow. Dale explained things to me in a way that was different from any other man. He was patient and didn't assume I knew anything or everything on the subject. His explanations were as clear as the stream that runs through this land.

A pier is a type of block foundation, a piece of concrete in the shape of a frustrum, or triangle with its top sawed off. Dale told me you can buy them or make them yourself out of boards built as molds to pour the liquid cement into a hard

Sill logs (tamarack) are re-barred on to piers (each pier 3–4 sacks cement) five feet apart.

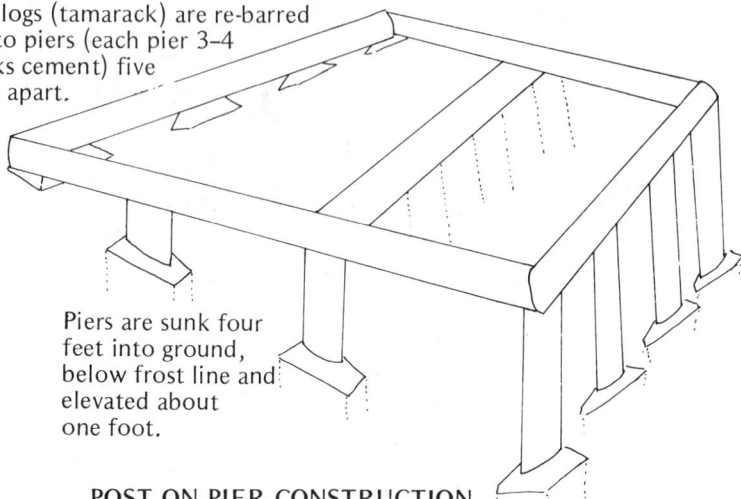

Piers are sunk four feet into ground, below frost line and elevated about one foot.

POST ON PIER CONSTRUCTION

CUTTING OUT WINDOWS AND DOORS

shape. On top of the pier you can place your foundation logs. The pier and log can either be sunk in the ground or rested on top. This type of foundation, Dale explained, is both practical and simple. I think I've decided to use the pier method.

Next, Dale told me about framing a window or doorsill in the log cabin. The easiest way is to build the cabin, then saw out the windows and door, framing them in with boards nailed to the logs. Before you saw, though, you should shove wedges of wood between the log cracks so all the logs do not fall down.

Dale also told me how to pipe water down to my cabin from the creek.

Step 1: Clear a pool in the creek and cover the bottom with a sheet of plastic.

Step 2: Sink a pipe underground into this plastic-covered pool.

Step 3: Connect the other pipe in a straight fashion and add sufficient linkage to allow the water to flow by gravity to the cabin. Always make sure your pipe is in a straight line; the water will lose momentum if the pipe

Plastic pool

Pipe to cabin

23

has a bend in it. In the wintertime, water could collect in the curves and freeze, thus shattering the pipe.

Dale asked me to share his bread and cheese with him. His eyes lit up with yellow suns when I said, "Yes." The bread Chris had made from ground soybeans and wheat berries in a cast-iron skillet. It was brown and yellow, with a crust resembling the tops of chocolate-covered coconut cookies. I had one piece of the chewy, satisfying bread and was full. That was pretty amazing, as my appetite was as huge as the sky-scraping pines towering above us. I asked him for the recipe, which is very simple and can be cooked over an open campfire.

BREAD

1 tbsp. yeast in 2¼ cups warm water
Rest in warm place 30 minutes
Add flour until thick enough to knead
Put mixture in oiled skillet over fire until firm
Flip bread when half done back into re-oiled skillet
Cook until solid.

Dale and I walked down the mountain after surveying the forest; he was amazed by the wealth of trees. We parted company where the path down to the old cabin begins and his trail leads over the hillsides to his parked car two miles away. He will come again Saturday morning at eight, and we will begin to fell trees for the cabin with a chain saw I will buy somewhere in town this week.

I whistled my way through the meadow, swinging my newly christened hatchet. I was happy after a full day's work. I thought about two weeks ago when work meant driving my little green cubicle of a car on an asphalt snake with all the other cubicle cars. Once at my destination I would ricochet around inside other cubicles for eight to ten hours before re-entering my little green car cubicle and driving home bumper to bumper. The only rush competing with me now is the creek sound.

Back at camp, Jean wasn't in a very happy frame, physically or mentally. I held her and told her about my workday with Dale and pressed my cold nose into her neck, which

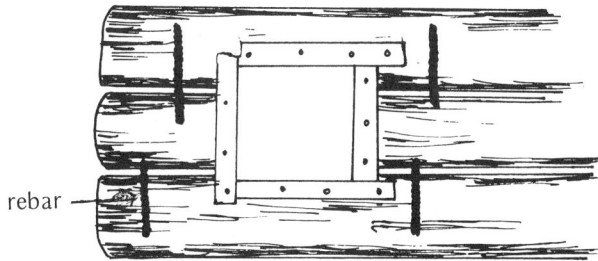

Rebar has been pounded
through logs around
area to be cut out.

Brace area to be cut out
with boards. Make sure
boards are straight and
level. Use inside of board
as saw guide

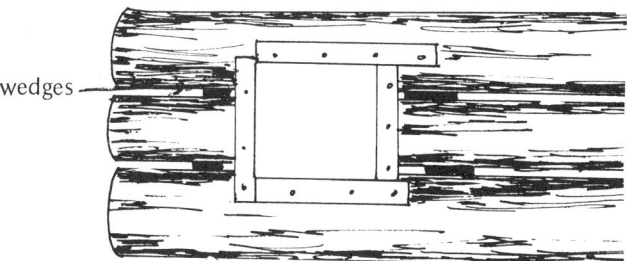

rebar

After logs are cut out
pound wedges between
cracks so logs will not
shift.

Remove braces and
finish trimming.

wedges

CUTTING A WINDOW

made goose bumps rise from every inch of her uncovered skin.

I strapped my empty pack onto my back and walked over
the mountain to the jeep. Took an alternate route and discovered rose hips—rose hips—rose hips—not speckled on bushes
but solid and cherry red over an entire mountain slope. I
picked handfuls until my hands were scratched and bleeding
from the guarding thorns.

At the jeep I unloaded the top carrier of its too-heavy-for-
me-to-lift trunks. I split my index fingernail lengthwise when
I fell from the top. My pack filled with a 12-pound Dutch
oven, spices, books, and some legumes, I headed back to the
old cabin and a supper of bean soup, which turned out to be
just plain beans.

Even up here on these rocks, high above the creek at a level with the pine tree tops, I can't get away from Tony. I had only hoped Jean and I could regain the ground our relationship once stood on before Tony comes out here to live with Jean. The plan is that Tony will come in July. They will live together somewhere on my land in the tipi Jean bought. I will live alone in my tent until the cabin is built and return to Minneapolis in September to go back to college. Tony and Jean will supposedly winter it up here. I wonder why I am extending my hospitality to them when it doesn't have anything to do with meeting my needs. I am keeping them in an environment near me, which doesn't help to lessen the intensity of my jealousy. I guess I still don't want to let go of Jean.

I don't hate Tony. I like him very much. I resent him when he is with Jean. I resent Jean when she is with Tony. I try not to make their love for each other hurt me, but it does because I don't share this love with anyone, not even Jean anymore. I have told myself over and over it is only good that they love each other, that it shouldn't concern me. Jean has told me this also. But I can't abide by these thoughts, as I am in continual turmoil and waste countless hours thinking about that which should not concern me. I want to forget Tony, forget Jean in order to save myself.

I woke this morning to Jean coming through the warped cabin door. I didn't even have to ask; I knew she had returned from the jeep where she had listened to a tape Tony sent her yesterday. I watched her from my sleeping bag take off her red pack, hoping she would start a fire to warm the cabin and make coffee. She sat down in the dusty green rocker, rolled a cigarette, and wrote a reply to Tony.

I lay in the sleeping bag, contemplating suicide or running away. Suicide was out, as I've weathered more turmoil than this before. So was running away, because this is my home and I cannot run away from a hurt that will always be.

Yesterday in town we visited Josie and Fred. Our conversation topics were protein, exercise, vegetarianism, deer poaching, new life styles, and Eckankar, which they are followers of. In the background Checo, their myna bird, kept repeating phrases he had learned. "Happy New Year, Merry

Christmas," a fake cough, and "God-Damn-You-Son-of-a-Bitch" filtered freely into our more relevant conversation.

I bought a chain saw in town, a McCulloch 10-10, weighing 15 pounds, with a 20-inch blade. It has a newly rebuilt engine because it blew up on its original owner, who could not afford to get it out of hock after it had been fixed. I lugged the saw and a full gas can over the mountain—not my idea of a good time, but it had to be done and I am the only one to rely on.

When we were up on the mountain, Dale told me gory stories of people severed by these motorized blades. A few years back, when he was logging with a friend, his friend's bar got pinched between the trunk of the tree he was sawing and flew back and cut his head off. Dale was one of the luckies who carried the head back down the mountain. I am afraid to use the chain saw.

We stopped at the Johnson's, the Mormon neighbors four miles below my land, to borrow a winch on the way home from town. Will is a man in his forties, with a bad back and six children. This family all clumped together in a two-room log cabin has seen some pretty hard times. Last year Will fell into a ditch and had to have surgery on his back, and Dorothy, his wife, went bankrupt with her bakery. Even though they have a deficit of money, they are rich in love. I showed Will my new chain saw, and he showed me the scar on his forehead from a bouncing blade.

I could write more, but my hand is freezing, and from where I sit on a rock this morning, escaping Jean, I see smoke rising from the cabin. Because it is cold and beginning to snow, I am forced inside with Jean.

Inside the cabin I go about wordlessly preparing my breakfast. Jean sits in the rocker, sharpening her hatchet. The honing of steel grates the silence between us. There is a dam of words—the only sounds, a faint crackle of fire, snowy winds, a file scraping metal.

Evening. The dam of words has been shattered by alternatives and decisions spoken. I was up on the mountain stripping bark from the tipi poles with a spud, a tool new in my crafty vocabulary. Jean came up and opened the flood gates. She needed reaffirming that she would feel comfortable on this land even though we would discontinue our relationship

from what it had been in the past. The slap in the face I knew had been coming for a long time when she let out the words, "Tony makes me happier, and I love him more than you."

The ground swam. The forest became a backdrop seen through a sheet of teary cellophane. My body remained as immobile as the logs I stared down at. Tears just slide down my face, and I could not move. My tears embedded themselves along with the other depressions made by snow dripping off the pine needles overhead. We talked little. I picked up my hatchet, exchanged a few more words, we embraced, and I walked down the mountain alone, not looking back, sobbing. The scene would have made a million at the box office, but unfortunately this was not a movie, and the only profit, more experience in the true-to-life drama of Yvonne Mary Pepin.

I walked for three hours, just thinking. I don't know what I'll do when Tony comes in two months. To put this situation in a rational perspective: I should just chalk up this relationship with Jean as one in a long line of lovers to come. But I can't let go of my feelings for her easily.

✝ April 27

So much has happened—more than I can record in the remaining light of this Sunday. Jean and I are still on rocky footing, with an occasional foothold. Half an hour ago we were yelling at each other; now she just left me from an embrace.

Dale came over the mountain, being blown about with the snow, to do his first day's work. Thinking we would start right up the mountain to fell trees was a grand display of my inexperience. For the next three hours Dale and I discussed cabin-building plans. I never realized building entailed so much forethought. Dimension after measurement, he made me go through and decide for myself every step of the cabin's construction. I know now which beam goes where, how to set sill logs and support them on piers. I know that rafters hold the roof up and joists support the floorboards.

The cabin I will build, a 20' x 15' structure, will have seven feet of clearance from the bottom floor to the loft floor. The loft walls will be four feet before the rafters are notched down. Twenty-two rafters will hold the roof secure; five joists will take care of the loft floor. The gable roof I have decided on will allow enough of a slope to keep on snow for insulation, but provide enough slant so the accumulation won't be too heavy. Twenty piers, which we will mold ourselves, will hold my log house up.

Just as we were preparing to head up the mountain, Mark and Brad came for a visit. The four of us went up, and Dale and I were lumberjacks. I chose the trees to fell, and Dale began cutting. It was fascinating to watch the majestically tall pine fall to the forest floor with a crash of branches and rain of needles. I tried to cut the second tree down, but only had the strength in my arms to make the upper cut. Dale explained the three cuts to make in the butt before felling a tree.

Cutting with this 15-pound whirling machine was not as easy for me as it was for Dale. When I got to the point where my quivering arms could no longer hold the saw, my sawdust-coated throat would yell for Dale, who would come and finish the fell, sawing in two minutes what it would take me ten to saw. Anything I would do, Dale could do in a fraction of

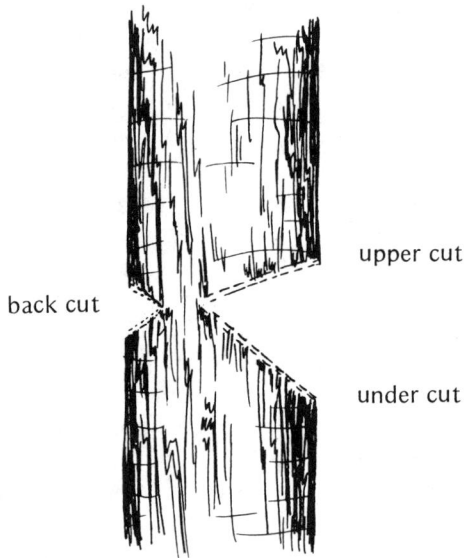

back cut

upper cut

under cut

the time. By the end of the day we had felled and limbed eight trees. I am so sore it hurts to breathe.

Mark and Brad stayed for a sweat. Mark prepared the sweat lodge, Brad cleaned the cabin, Jean washed dishes, and I prepared the day's feast of pea and lentil soup, and baked a pan of soy and wheat bread flavored with coffee and honey.

The sweat went well. Mark had covered the floor of the lodge with pine boughs so we wouldn't freeze our butts on the snow. Everyone but Jean ran through the snow and jumped, steaming, into the creek. I washed my hair in the ice-flowing stream. Now I know why the Swedes have such strong hearts from saunas and cold water. If you didn't, you would die of shock.

We all had a long talk after dinner. Brad wants to help me build my cabin while also working on Mark's. Mark said, "You either help me all the time or not at all." Brad is now staying here to help me build all summer if I can feed him. It will be nice to have another set of muscles, but I'm unsure whether or not I can keep him in grub.

✛ April 28

By quitting time today, Dale had felled twenty-seven trees, I had limbed them. I smashed my hand black and blue on a pine tree.

Since becoming a woman lumberjack, I have, besides developing my muscles with all this exercise, developed an appetite. I have been eating three large meals a day, and a slight bulge has accumulated beneath my long underwear where my once-flat abdomen occupied space.

✛ April 29

I think my late-night writing would benefit if I had the proper illumination to write by. One candle and some narrow light cast by the open grate of the cookstove do not suffice. Hot running water and electricity are what I miss most about civilization

I write tonight with a bloody and smashed index finger, a bruised and swollen kneecap, sore arms and back, and a slightly sunburned face. I put in nine hours of work on the mountain without a break. Dale didn't show for work until noon, so I went up alone to finish limbing. I had a wonderful time by myself, working while planning the cabin and landscaping in my mind.

On a downswing of the axe my finger was wedged between the tool handle and the tree. I could only grit my teeth and hang limp over the log I'd been limbing. The pain was so intense I couldn't even let out the phrase "Son of a Bitch" that was running through my head. I knew my finger had been smashed good when blood began to seep through the new $4.95 pair of leather work gloves.

I pulled my finger out and took one look before I fainted. It was as if an ocean wave of tiny crackling bubbles passed full force over me. I came to, to see a pool of blood drips collecting in the white snow beneath the bloody cavern surrounding my exposed knuckle. I thought, "What kind of lumberjack am I when I faint at a wound as small as a finger?"

I stood up from the log I had draped my collapsing body over, took another look at the wound the color of roses swelling over an exposed layer of white fat, and fainted again, this time backwards across the stump the tree had towered down from.

I don't know how long I'd been passed out, but I was revived by the sound of chopping wood. I yelled out

my long "Yoo-hoo," which was greeted by "Good morning, Yvonne." When I went over to find Dale, he looked at me and said I was looking a little pale.

We cut and limbed thirty-one trees and cut twenty-six of these into lengths. We measured and sawed fourteen 22' logs and twelve 16' logs. I wanted to finish up the five other trees lying on the ground, but tripped and slammed my knee onto a branch knob. I could only roll in the snow and yell "Shit," the pain was so bad. Dale ran over to see if I had killed myself. This is when I decided to quit, because if I didn't, I would probably run an axe blade into my head.

When we parted trails at the mountain, Dale said, "Goodbye, boss, you're a hard-working man." This was a lot, coming from Dale, saying I was hard working and all, but I didn't know whether to take his reference to my gender as a cut or a compliment.

✝ May 1, 1975

Naked as the wind under blue Pine Valley sky, I eat soybeans and write. This is the first day I have been able to shed my entire eight layers of clothes comfortably. I discover many marks of my new trade—bruises and cuts. I have spent most of the day reading, writing, and drawing. Now I must sharpen the chain saw and tote it up the mountain to cut tipi poles and logs. Jean has been very cold to me the last two days, and I am becoming tired of communicating with a rock.

Evening. The campfire roars next to me, as does the bitterness and rage inside of me that burns more powerfully every day. Our relationship on an hour-to-hour basis is like a roller coaster over ice and fire. I am not as happy as I should be when she is around. I always feel as if I've done something to offend her.

I had ideally thought that this time spent away from the city, away from Tony, would give us the opportunity to grow closer. It has done the opposite. Every day the growing gulf between us diminishes our love further. I don't know what to do. I feel like abandoning this land to Jean and leaving the turmoil behind, with all my plans and dreams.

Our relationship is so dead now we had sex the other night

out of boredom. The love I had for Jean is becoming blacker and blacker as the days we spend together scorch it crisp. How do I get out before this love is cinder and ash?

✙ May 2

I am beside another smoldering campfire in the morning, writing and drinking coffee while saw-whet owls play music for me. Jean has gone up the mountain to strip tipi poles. It is certainly less hectic writing with proper illumination. At night, when I usually write, my train of thought is always being interrupted by having either to dump off excess candle-wax or poke and kindle the fire, and a train of thought is hard enough for me just to hold long enough to run it down on paper.

The day before I left Metro, Barbara Bush, my literature teacher, told me in front of the entire class that I would never be an intellectual because I couldn't understand the ideas of the authors from whose texts I read and I couldn't hold a thought or idea in my head. She made me feel very stupid and inferior because she had intellectual ability and I did not. I didn't tell her, though, my definition of an intellectual is a "fancy bullshitter." I don't feel stupid anymore. I am here, and she is in her nine-to-four office job, wishing she were here.

I dreamed last night I was working in a factory; I think it was the toy factory where I worked the summer I was sixteen, filling boxes behind an assembly line. Boxes were spaced about one quarter inch apart on the conveyer belt, and the women filled them with multi-colored toy parts.

In the dream it was time for the 10 A.M. coffee break. With my free ten minutes, I was going down the street from the factory to buy a chain saw at a hardware store.

All the clerks in the store were men with dead-codfish-colored faces. They all wore black suits. I asked where the chain saws were, and the dead-codfish-faced clerk looked at me doubtfully. He pointed past a display of colorful shoes, more shoes in more colors than I had ever seen before. I decided to buy a pair of bright blue running shoes to wear when I went for naked runs in the mountains. I asked the cod-faced clerk to get them for me. He said I couldn't have them because they were blue and on a shelf too high for me to reach them. He reached up, took them down, and sold them to a man behind me.

The cod-faced man in the chain saw department thought I was kidding when I told him I wanted to buy a chain saw. He wanted to sell me fingernail polish instead. I persisted. I came for a chain saw. He pulled down two identical yellow cases. I opened them up. The chain saws were made out of carved marble with gold leaf ornamentation, like a lamp my mother had purchased for our house months before she died. I told the fish-faced man these would never serve my purpose. He laughed, and I hurried back to work.

Walking down the street, I saw all the other women hurry to their positions on the assembly line. Their faces were blank, and they all wore scarves tied around their heads. I looked at all the women and yelled, "It's 10:10, and all the females in the world must get back to work!"

In the lunchroom at noon break, a pimply-faced boy sat opposite me in a booth. He said he could kick a 220-foot ponderosa pine over with his bare foot. All the blank-faced women turned to the boy and gave him "Help me" looks.

We had a meeting with the men who ran the factory. They also had codfish faces and wore black suits. They agreed to release all the women and the pimply-faced boy from the factory if he could kick over the 220-foot ponderosa pine with his bare foot.

All the women sat on one side of the stadium. The cod-faced men in their emotionless black suits occupied the other half. The women held gray rags. The pimply-faced boy and I were in the middle of the ring beside a ponderosa pine with a base of six feet in diameter.

The boy removed his shoes and took a few practice kicks in the air, then went straight for the tree. His leg crumpled like an accordion. He fell back, his face now the color of cod. The tree laughed. Two big men put the boy on a stretcher and carried him away—I did not know where.

I looked up and saw the women on one side, the cod-faced men on the other. The next thing I knew I was being grabbed on my upper arm by a huge gray hand. Then I was standing on a jagged rock in the middle of a gray ocean underneath a black sky. I awoke from the dream to the sounds of Annabelle's claws pulling on the faded green rocking chair.

✝ May 3

Stayed in the bag until 10:30 this morning. The only reason to get up was to arrange pans under rain rivulets running through the roof and onto the floor, or to shut the door continually being blown open by the storm raging outside. I got out of the bag once to reposition pans and twice to move my books, which were in the firing line of the raindrop bombardment. Jean and I stayed inside all day and baked.

In the evening the rain and snow had let up, and I set out to dig drain ditches across the road, or Will, who is going to come up here with his cat next week to drag the logs, would get sunk in the muddy ruts. I dug the first ditch perpendicular to the road and watched all the rain built up in puddles fill this trough and cascade over the hillside. I felt proud of my ingenious achievement.

I dug seven of these ditches; later I am to hear them called "water boxes." I was digging ditches because it had to be done; no one told me they had to be dug, I just knew. No one to dig them but me. At times the shovel would suck deep into the mud and pull out with a huge smacking sound that reminded me of two lips. All the time I dug in falling snow. The mountains, bushes, and I looked as if we had been powdered in sugar.

When I walked home in the dark, I could hear bullfrogs croaking in the snowstorm.

In *A Room of One's Own,* Virginia Woolf describes creamy pudding, partridge, boiled potatoes, wine, etc., as the fuel to kindle the light in one's spine. That is fine for a college campus, but on a snowy night in the mountains, those delicacies stand punily next to coffee and corn bread running warm with falls of butter and honey.

✝ May 4

Two inches of snow greeted me this morning. I dug more ditches and, even greater than the trough that drains away winter, made a decision that will affect my life more than run-off: in June, I will not live with Jean anymore.

I cannot and will not live with this daily turmoil. I will live alone on a grassy spot in a tent near the creek, below the building site on my land. It is time I start growing again. I must learn to live alone and not feel lonely. To become aware of myself more and to feel whole with my surroundings are steps in my growing no institution will teach me, but what I must learn from the experience of solitude. I need hours alone with my thoughts—writing and drawing—to understand a part of me lost or never discovered.

✝ May 5

If I were to base the turn of circumstances in my life on meaningful coincidence, then perhaps because of some universal thread connecting me with my destiny, I began reading Thoreau's *Walden* this morning after making my decision yesterday to live alone.

This man's words, even though sexist and arrogant, do give me insight into living alone with nature. I will converse with bullfrogs and trout instead of my bumbling communications with Jean. Without opening my mouth, I will talk with the woodland creatures, and they will know what I am saying. I also wish to learn to express myself on paper—my true feelings and intent. I want to conquer my inability to express myself through this awkward form of writing—struggling with content, punctuation, syntax, and spelling. I want to discontinue the feeling of being rushed to expel the seep behind the plaster block of my brain.

Jean was in a mood today as bitter as this weather. I had to stir the shit in the shitter and spread lime over it this afternoon. Stirring shit is not like stirring a light pudding confection. I broke off in the shit the pine branch I had been using to distribute the shit in all corners of the outhouse's underneath. I felt nauseous the entire time and humored myself

while sprinkling lime on top of the shit by imagining I was sprinkling powdered sugar over a giant brownie I had just spread into a pan. However, I ran from the outhouse with a tide of vomit rising in my throat. Next time the shit needs distributing, I'll let someone else take a turn.

I found wild scallions on the mountainside today. I gathered more rose hips. The thorns reminded me of Jean—if I reached to pick the fruit without a sharp wit about me, I got pricked by the thorn guards.

Jean still isn't talking to me. I asked her why, and she replied, "I don't have anything to say," yet she spends half the day writing letters to Tony. We are down to one candle, then the only resort is bed. I don't know if I can lie beside her tonight, feeling the way I do. I am so tired of feeling I've done something to warrant punishment from her. Oh, fuck it! I've spent enough time remorsing over an ice slab.

Tonight I write by proper but mechanical illumination: I have fixed the broken Coleman. What a treat to see the hand pushing the pen.

I awoke after sunrise and got up, despite the cold, because I could not tolerate another morning of waking to Diane's silent chill. Still wiping the sleep from my eyes, I took an early morning walk. I imagined finding some deer horns before going to sleep last night, and behold, this morning in my wide pathway, I found not one but a pair of ebony gray elk horns. The points bore a total of twelve. An elk horn in each hand, I continued my walk and scaled a pillar of serpentine and granite. From this mountain mast, I was able to see not only the flowing Pine Valley valley but also the saddle of my land, the looming Strawberries behind still covered in snow. Through the flannel-eyes filter of my early morning vision, I spied a deer. The white of its tail was followed by the whites of my eyes as it moved up and down in graceful hops over obstacles of juniper and rock.

Back at the cabin, Jean grunted something about going to town to mail Mother's Day cards. I hastily ate breakfast and went to pick wild scallions for Josie.

On the drive home today, Jean and I talked heatedly about our present living situation. She is thinking about sending for Tony sooner than July and wanted to know if I thought she would be using me for this land. This statement came a few sentences after she said she enjoyed this country and my land more than me.

What am I supposed to think? To decide? I know Jean and the good in her, and I want those characteristics to outweigh the negative ones I'm feeling now, I know Tony and also acknowledge that his positive attributes must outweigh the more dismal ones I've construed in my jealousy.

At the cabin, I unpacked from town and went walking. My thinking became jumbled with the pace my feet were trying to set, so I sat down to rest on a rock. From there I could see the sunset. In order to sort out my problems, I needed to see myself. I needed a mirror and resorted to the ever-faithful pen and paper. I made a list of the things I see wrong with me. I had to stop writing at a quarter of one hundred, as my problems are indefinite.

✛ **May 7**

Part II In Yvonne Grows Up

Amber fell
the drop
the tear drop
from my eye
to her shoulder
smooth
descending
a minute
waterfall
down her breast.

I am alone. There is not a human being for four miles. I am Yvonne Mary Pepin, a young woman living alone in a remote mountain saddle. Jean left a few hours ago, left her new life, Annabelle, and me, to return to Minnesota, where she will find in Tony what I would not give her.

The continuous hurt had to stop. We decided the best thing for our relationship was to part, in hopes that what love we still have for one another is not poisoned. Maybe the distance we will share now in miles will help us see the more positive aspects of each other, of our relationship.

She left, she said, for three weeks. She will return with Tony. Jean has Tony, a human, to fill her needs. I have this land and myself. I will miss the warmth and touch of another human, but feel this time alone will allow me the opportunity to become more independent with myself and surroundings.

Our good-bye today was filled with the genuine caring that two people who love one another share. We held each other tightly and cried. Tears would fall, subside, then flow again as we caressed each other's face, hair, half-naked body in the Oregon sun.

Jean strapped her pack over her back and walked away from me. I watched her red pack bob up and down over the mountainside.

The shadows grow long tonight and flow in dark shapes over the land. It would be a lie to say I am not afraid. I am not afraid of wild life or injury but of the uncertainty darkness holds. I have heard "You have nothing to fear but fear itself." I will repeat this over and over on those nights when it is dark outside and my imagination takes hold, creating rapists, crazy men, moans, screams, and bands of drunken hunters scouring the wilderness in search of me. My imagination feeds in the night. I fear the male human animal more than I fear the coyote, bear, or bobcat.

The hardest part of this night will come inside my sleeping bag, whose mate has unzipped itself and is now, I imagine, lying in the jeep, traveling through Idaho. Almost every night for the past two years I have been held by, or have held, another warm body in my sleep. Tonight I will hold myself.

She had to go
into the night
as I have to learn to
hold my night. .

✝ May 8

Waking alone was not the dreaded experience I had imagined but one of feeling wholesome in myself. I dressed hurriedly, then walked up the mountainside to dig more ditches, singing with the birds in the bright morning. I was happy, happy Jean was gone and I was here with myself. The mud was so deep in one section of the road it grabbed one of my new $6.95-a-pair rubber boots and sucked it off.

In the afternoon I had my art lesson. A cloud study was appropriate as they billowed overhead in cotton clusters. My assignment: to portray the cumulus with watercolor, incorporating color, texture, and tonality. I finished this, then a pen and ink of pine and rock. Then I went up the mountain to drawknife trees.

This was my first try with a drawknife, and I struggled to pull the blade that would slice the bark off the tree. I felt muscle taxations in my shoulders, hands, sides, and back. It started to rain, and I headed back to the cabin, stiff with pine sap.

✛ May 9

My back, arms, legs, and head serve no purpose tonight except to hinder my once healthy body. It is not even dusk when I am driven into the cabin because of chill. My hands show their labors in ant-infested manure, dark earth, pine sap, hot and ice cold water, and countless other elements that taint my flesh.

I walked up the mountain with the rising sun to drawknife until noon, when I returned to the old cabin and began to build a greenhouse. It was hot out, and I wore only cut-offs. I imagine I looked comical carrying tubs of manure across the creek. All day under the sun I worked at filling pots with a mixture of manure and dark dirt. Into this I pushed down tiny seeds. The greenhouse I made from willow branches lashed in arches and covered with sheets of plastic.

Inside the greenhouse I placed boards over bricks to elevate the potted plants. In the afternoon the temperature inside is above 90, in the morning around 50 degrees.

✛ May 10

I awoke this morning in the same state I went to bed in—chills, aches, and weakness. I knew I was ill enough to seek medical attention, which I did by beginning the four-mile walk to the neighbors. I met the Doc in his meadow, and he offered to take me to the hospital after I told him my symptoms, which he thought might be Rocky Mountain spotted tick fever.

I had the Doc drive me to Dorothy's because I thought she might know what was wrong with me, owing to her experience raising kids. She called the clinic, and the doctor said to come in and get checked out. To do this I had to walk down the county road five miles, then hope to hitch a ride from the highway into town. Dorothy and her daughter wanted to drive me into town, but couldn't because their car had a flat tire. I began the walk. Every step I took created painful throbs in my head, back, and knees. As I walked my only thought was of wanting to be wrapped in a blanket and rocked. Even though my fever was hotter than the sun on my back, I was shaking with cold.

Over my shoulder I saw dust from an approaching car I thought I could thumb a ride into town from. It was Dorothy. She had fixed her flat and come to take me to the hospital. In town the doctor performed professional tests on me and, from the results, wanted me to spend the next two days in the hospital. I said nix, knowing the sterile, drug-induced healing offered by hospitals. It seemed inferior to my method of fasting, sweating, resting, and flushing myself with rose hip tea. I agreed to be hospitalized only if my temperature of 102 degrees was to rise another degree.

I had lunch at the Johnson's; my protesting did me no good. I tried to tell Dorothy that they had already been too kind to me. Dorothy listened to my protest with closed ears, saying that, "When one is sick, one needs to be taken care of."

After the Johnsons brought me home, I fell asleep outside in the sun on a blanket. I was awakened by a soft hand on my hot head. It was Josie. She had heard I was ill and came to check on me. Later, Brad returned from Washington after retrieving his carpenter tools, and it looks as if he will spend the summer up here working with me. So much for my reclusivity. I drank pots of rose hip tea today and flushed my fever down to 100 degrees.

✝ May 11

I am still too weak to work. I feel helpless as a new-born baby. Even to chop a tiny bit of wood today wore me out.

44

Brad made a sweat for me, which I sat in for over an hour, broken only by several plunges into the creek. The heat and steam helped to ooze this sickness through the pores of my skin.

✚ May 12

My strength is such that my arms behave like licorice whips when I tried to dig with a shovel this morning. I regretfully resign myself during this sickness to the labors only of my thoughts.

I thought about Jean today—how I miss her or haven't missed her since she left. I have been content and at ease with myself twenty-four hours of the day. I have never before in the eighteen years of my life felt so satisfied with myself.

What does this mean, to love someone but not miss them? Does it mean that it is not love at all but a dependency overcome.

✚ May 14

Beans, rice, and bread. Rice, beans, and bread. Starch, starch, and more starch. I crave the green, orange, and red of a fresh vegetable salad. Since Brad has come, my budget for food, meant to accommodate only my appetite, has had to expand to encompass Brad's hunger.

The two-pound ration of cheese I purchased last week, which would suffice me for two weeks, was down to the level a starving mouse could not be satisfied with only three days after I brought it home from the store. The bag of apples I brought home the same day, which would also last me for two weeks, is now down to only three of the luscious red, mineral-packed fruits my teeth love to puncture and gnash.

My body weeps for the roughage it thrives on because of the starch it must digest. Last night I made two loaves of bread, and tonight there is only half a loaf left. Brad has downed the rest, except for two small pieces inside of me.

Saturday, when I go to town, I will devour with my eyes the produce section—lettuce dripping with water, apples glowing red, green, and yellow, tomatoes and carrots, and oh, the broccoli. I will leave them all in their refrigerator cases and reluctantly saunter over to the aisle of beans, rice, and bread, since my pocketbook for one must stretch to buy food for two.

Brad and I stripped ten logs today, a record for us so far. I am getting better, and my strength continues to build after the sickness. I worked the entire afternoon without my shirt on; my chest is black with sap, my hair so stiff it resembles a plastic wig.

We worked for eight hours, the blade pulling through wet dark bark and revealing the white pureness of the log underneath. When one side of the log had been stripped, it had to be rolled over and the other side begun. It is no easy task to roll a wet 22-foot log, and my muscles could muster only a fraction of the strength to do the job. I relied on Brad and his muscles. Now I know why he eats so much.

I rested between two freshly drawknifed logs, spinning a piece of bark between my lips, with my hair tied up in a bun, my shirt open to expose my breasts spackled with pitch, my jeans stiff with sap also. Brad came by and said *Seventeen* magazine needs me to promote the natural look.

✛ May 15

I feel empty tonight, like a pot waiting to be filled with warm water. I miss being close to someone, sharing touch. Is this an inovert form of missing Jean? How will I know if it is just her shell I miss or the contents inside the shell?

In less than two weeks I will be nineteen. I feel the responsibilities of my youth. The existential me is being suppressed by the material me. I dream about taking my sketch pad and just blowing with the winds to draw the crannies of this country. I feel my fortune, though, in having things come easily to me, like this land, a gift of my parents and purchased because of my need for a home.

Brad has a freedom I envy. He has no money and just drifts around, working occasionally or helping people with their work in exchange for room and board. Brad is wealthy in his freedom.

✢ May 16

One month away from the city tonight, I celebrate by watching the orange ball of sun descend behind the mountain crest. One month ago, at this very hour, I was driving through South Dakota with a woman I thought I needed. During this month I have found answers to many of my questions, finding what I need inside myself. Today, half the logs to build my home are cut and peeled. My garden, incubating in the greenhouse, is sprouting premature seeds. I have already carved my life into this mountain. The center of my life I thought I had such a desperate need for has removed herself from my immediate presence and left me to find my true center, inside myself.

Dale and Sophie came up the mountain today. He had heard from Mark that I had taken ill and came to check on me.

After they left, I began to mark more trees to fell. I heard an unfamiliar "Yoo-hoo" and let out a "Yee-haw" to indicate my presence in the obscurity of my wooded locale. I saw a man in a green shirt with a skinny dog come bursting through the trees.

"There you are, you good-looking hunk of a woman," said Frank Miller, a man I met once before in town. He owns the building supply store. He had also heard I'd been sick and came to visit me. Frank is in his mid-forties, with a wife and five children.

Ten minutes into our conversation, Frank commented on how pale I was looking, and two minutes later I fainted. He caught me before I fell into the branches. I guess I was not as completely recovered from my illness as I thought. I felt like a fool, fainting in front of Frank.

✢ May 18

Mark drove me to Bend on a buying trip in his little green Datsun. We smoked bowl after bowl of dope, chased by joint

47

after joint. I screamed on and off the entire drive as Mark took the sharp, steep curves at 75 mph.

In Redmond, we stopped at an A & W for lunch. While we waited for our order I read *Lesbian Connections*. Mark told me to put it down, because people would see me through the cab and think I was weird. Those words no more than came out of his mouth than an old beat-up woody station wagon pulled up alongside of us, driven by a fat old man wearing a Mickey Mouse hat, the kind with big black ears.

Mark and I each bought wood cookstoves to the tune of $336 apiece. The stoves have a lifetime guarantee. I bought a work hat at Penney's for me and some gloves for Brad. I rode buckboard on the shopping cart Mark pushed through Safeway while singing "I Want to Get Married." Mark cut melons into Dream Cycle colored wedges on the drive home. We smoked six more joints and sang the "Fish Cheer" to the barren landscape between mouthfuls of chocolate chip cookies. I found a new friendship with Mark that day.

We arrived in Pine Valley at 7 P.M. and were filling up at the Arco station when we met Pete, the 34-year-old barber of this town. He is a pill-popping, dope-smoking cowboy type, with emphasis on the "boy." Pete had heard about some "chick" building a log cabin up Dean Creek, and when he learned I was the "chick," he invited Mark and me over to his trailer to smoke some dope and meet his "chick."

I replied, "Yes, I would like to get stoned, peep, peep, because you're such a generous cock, peep, peep, and I would like to see your roost, peep, peep, and meet your 'chick,' peep, peep." Mark looked on, a little pale. Pete didn't call me "chick" anymore.

Pete's trailer, on the outskirts of town, was loaded with cheap sex trinkets and plastered with girly pin-ups. Karen, the woman he lives with, greeted me with a spaced out "Hi." She looked like a hallucinating ostrich egg underneath her black bush of an Afro.

Pete put four lids into Karen's hands and said, "Roll, Baby." Karen obediently sat in a chair, dispensed the lids' contents onto a magazine, and rolled the joints, which were retrieved by Pete's outstretched, expectant hand. He gave me a three-foot-high bong, with the instructions to pack it full with as few seeds as possible.

The four of us smoked and drank beer until five cowboy types entered through the trailer's open door. I had just exhaled the contents of the bong when my slightly disoriented perceptions concluded "cowboys-rednecks." I hurriedly hid the bong between my legs and waited for a fight.

Surprise. Surprise. My stereotype of a cowboy was shattered when Pete offered the oldest of the five, a man in his mid-fifties, a joint. While the bong made the rounds, the youngest cowboy passed a paper-bag-covered bottle of alcohol. Pete and I stood in the circle of cowboys, but they never handed us the bottle.

I asked for a drink. The youngest cowboy apologized for not offering me the bottle in the first place, saying he thought women only wanted to be offered cigars. This provoked the other cowboys into hee-hawing, knee-slapping laughter. I nonchalantly tipped the paper-bagged whiskey bottle to my lips and held it there while I took three big gulps. I made sure all the cowboys saw me drink and watched my Adam's apple swallow in three movements. They all, including Karen, kept steady eyes on me, and I nonchalantly passed the bottle. It was hard determination, a shoving down of the senses, that allowed me not to let my eyes water from the whiskey burning in me.

The cowboy across from me started making cracks about women not knowing their places, trying to egg me on into a conversation giving them more opportunity to make sexist jokes. I pretended not to notice and began to stomp my feet and sway with the music. I really did not care what the cowboys said; I was aware of their shallowness. I was not going to allow them to bait me into playing their game or to ruin the effects of my stone.

When Mark and I were leaving, the cowboy who had passed me the bottle apologized to my brother, thinking that it might have offended him. Mark replied that it was no concern of his, that I did what I wanted. As we walked out the door that old familiar sensation of body fatigue and an ocean of bubbles overpowered me, and I fainted into one of the cowboy's catch.

Semi-recovered five minutes later, I tried to explain it was not because of the whiskey or dope that I passed out, but I was recuperating from Rocky Mountain spotted tick fever. I tried to make another quick exit, but passed out again. To sum up the situation, I felt like a fool in front of these drawling, snickering, I-told-you-so cowboys, with emphasis on the "boys."

I left before Mark and squatted behind his truck to pee. While I was in the process of buttoning up my britches, all the cowboys came out and caught me in the act. They turned around in embarrassment and excused themselves. I said, "Quite all right. It happens all the time."

✝ May 19

Brad has joined Mark for the evening at his camp up Stonehill Creek to eat a stewed porcupine Mark shot. They could not sense my reason for not joining them, so I made the excuse that I must stay and wait for Annabelle to return, as she went off yesterday.

There is no way I could enjoy another evening with these two farting in unison or having fart and burp contests. I need to flush my entire system of them. They do bring me much joy and are my real companions here, but they lack the senses to understand the sensitive needs I have to express. When in the company of these two, my individuality subconsciously mixes with traits of their beings, and I blend into the pudding.

Brad and I are very synchronized companions; our characters and attitudes are agreeable. We are open and honest with one another. I have never been so at ease or enjoyed any man as much before. He is the first man I've been able to work well with.

But Brad and I are like the tide and the moon, pulling against each other in our physical differences. My five-foot, 99-pound composition is no match for his six-foot, 200-pound body. Our eating habits can be analogized with a sparrow and a hawk. Added to his eating habits, or a complement to them, are Brad's incessant farts. His anus is persistently expelling gas. A fart here and there doesn't bother me, but Brad never stops. I suppose it is healthy, but for whose air?

I doused a seven-foot-high pile of branches and limbs up on the mountain today with gasoline. I crawled up on the pile and lit a piece of newspaper to ignite the brush. No sooner had I dropped the match than an explosion of orange blew me right off the pile. I was singed, but that was all. Wiping the smelly burnt hair, once my eyebrows, from above my eyes, I contemplated my stupidity and vowed never to do that one again.

We burned brush all day, taking Smokey the Bear precautions to contain the flames. There are enough logs cut and peeled today to begin building. I have set June 1 as my goal to begin.

✝ May 21

Drawknifing, limbing, piling brush—my body is feeling stronger every day behind this work load. My pants are so stiff with pine sap they stand by themselves. I will have to soak them malleable again in some gasoline.

Annabelle has been gone for days now, I begin to think it is because of Brad's farting.

✝ May 24

The sun sets, ethereal behind the mountains, and a fist of shadows clenches the valley below. Sudden gusts rush pine needles gold with movement. In the dying light, I sit again on my granite perch above the cabin. I feel the need to be alone

with the wind, a friend to myself. I am absorbing all the colors, from dark-sap green pine to the faded purple of a flower past its season.

Brad woke this morning to the birthday signs I had taped up inside the cabin proclaiming the celebration of his twenty-fifth year on earth. We went into town to eat, shower, and shop. We went to lunch at a smorgasbord and smuggled extra pieces of chicken away in our backpack.

At the grocery store we bought essential provisions, especially Brad's eight-pound can of peanut butter. We left with our packs full of groceries, each carrying a tomato plant and drawing curious stares from passers-by. We sang "Taxi" as we walked down Main Street to the Pine Valley Motor Lodge to shower. We appeared half an hour later, clean, pink and smiling, dripping beads of water from our wet heads onto the street.

Late at night I stay awake with moon, with owl; we prey in the dark together. Moon is the light needed to stalk and kill whatever lies in owl's black night path. Owl is the master of the night and preys in the white ice of moonlight.

✝ May 25

Dale and family came to visit today. We all walked up the mountain and ate lunch while discussing building plans. We roughly surveyed the corners, marking them with boulders and measuring lines, with string pulled taut.

Brad and I walked over the mountain with the Parkers back to their truck. Sophie snagged her leg on a stick and began to cry, so I carried her on my back. Chris held Jud because he was too small to walk, and we walked behind the men. I felt domestic but content.

Brad and I stopped off at the Johnson's to borrow a winch and cable. We stood behind a barbed wire fence talking with Will and Sam, his brother. We talked about building, and they directed all the questions, or answers to the questions I would ask, to Brad. They didn't ever hear me when I made a statement. I got furious and went into the house to help Dorothy wash dishes. I scrubbed tomato sauce off plates in a rage of sexual injustice.

+ May 26

Began to winch logs out of the creek bed today. This is the most strenuous work I've done yet. I used every muscle in my body to its maximum and felt my bones pull tight up against my skin as I strained. It began to rain and we kept working, being drenched all afternoon. Tonight I have a sore throat and am exhausted. While I was washing my face in the aluminum pan tonight, my reflection reminded me to record the recipe for my newest bread.

BREAD

2 cups corn flour
1 cup soy flour
1 cup milk
1 cup powdered milk
Mix these ingredients together, then add:
Grated orange peel
Crushed rose hips
A couple of fistfuls of sunflower seeds
Cinnamon to taste
Speck of salt
Some dribbles of honey
Put mixture in oiled skillet
Place on a spit-sizzling-hot stovetop
Cook until firm, about 15 minutes
Flip bread when half done back into re-oiled skillet
Cook until solid, about 15 minutes

+ May 27

Stars stud a cold, clear night, fire burning orange, burning blue. I drink cheap Moselle in celebration on the eve before my nineteenth birthday. With every moment, my eyelids begin to ease close like brick jaws. My head grows lighter with every wine sip, yet I struggle to stay awake until the moment to celebrate. In one hour I will be nineteen.

Five feet one and 99 pounds on the feed scale in town last week. Yet life sometimes seems as complex and materialistic as someone's three times my age. I have played the stock market, own a car, pay insurance, am acquiring greater responsibility in building my own home. I have seen the deaths of my parents. I have fought the injustice of the judicial system —I could go on. There is much that makes me seem older than my nineteen-year design.

Brad fixed the winch while I went to scour the woods for a stray tree to drawknife. My search was interrupted by his loud and profuse swearing. I went back to find him hammering on the winch and throwing rocks to dispel his frustration. I offered my services and gently pushed into place the cable he had been beating on for thirty minutes that had frustrated him. We hugged each other with joy over our accomplishment. I joked about the winch just needing a woman's touch.

I would groan and grimace in pain as I cranked the winch's steel handle, with a log attached to the metal cable I turned around the spool. I have never used my muscles to this extent before. Even through the sweat and exhaustion I smiled because of the pure, clean joy of this activity. I was happy to expose new muscles and was joyously thinking about the day I would finally be sitting inside my cabin by the fire, the clean yellow logs smiling at me. I would know how my cabin had been built.

✝ May 28

No work this morning. I went up alone to the building site and reflected on the passing year, thinking back on my fifteenth birthday and my dream then of buying wilderness land and building a home. I sat on my imaginary porch and thought back to when I was preparing to leave Minnesota to search out west for land. I had just turned eighteen, was out to conquer the wilds of real estate, but hesitant about the adventure. Now, here I am today, my dream found and paid for in full, building onto my dream with real logs.

Josie came when the sun told us it was time to eat the carrot cake Brad had concocted that morning. Josie gave me her present and one sent up by Jill, the Doc's wife. We all took a sweat, though Josie wore her bathing suit. She surprised us by staying in the lodge longer than either Brad or me and submerging in the icy creek more times. She just kept saying, "Oh, how beautiful."

After Josie left, Brad and I lay in the sun, naked, and read mail Josie had brought over for us. Temptation drew me quickly from my letters to Brad's bare posterior, and I drew a big face, complete with ears, on his hairy, sunburned ass.

I had a long letter from Jean and a shorter one, both very emotional and proclaiming her love for me. The letters flamed up my desire for her and fanned my confusion over the whole affair. Just as I decide to end the close relationship with Jean, some turn of events makes me warm to her again. I am at constant odds over what to do.

Just as I was beginning to think Mark had forgotten my birthday, he came over the hill bearing presents—a bottle of whiskey, a *Playboy* magazine, a Buck hunting knife.

✝ May 29

I ran all over town today, wearing my sheer, embroidered western shirt and short cut-offs, my tan hairy legs sprouting from them. I connected with all the men who run the building trades. I bought a wheelbarrow, cement, rebar, rope, and some tools. In every store I had to explain what a "little gal" like me was going to do with these purchases. I was always the

center of a group of men when I had to explain the nature of my expenditures.

"I'm building a log cabin," I would profess proudly in the midst of their stares.

"With your husband?" they would ask.

I left the Pine Valley hardware store, pushing my new red wheelbarrow full of axe handles, rope, spikes, block and tackle, and other assorted implements of the trade. Pride beamed across my face as I caught my reflection in the windows, walking down Main Street behind my wheelbarrow.

Brad and I sat across from Josie's house on the church steps and broke our twenty-four-hour fast with a root beer float we made in a bucket—half a gallon of chocolate ice cream and two quarts of root beer. My stomach was ready to burst after this delicious breaking of a fast. I don't plan to do it again, though. I felt like exploding and groaned my way over to Josie's. She told me not to complain around her because "If one is to overindulge, one must do so silently." I suffered silently in Josie's doorway, watching her prepare supper. I felt at home.

Josie dropped Brad and me off at Fir Creek Road, and we pushed the wheelbarrow and contents up the mountain. It was hard work, but I enjoyed feeling my naked breasts bounce every time the wheelbarrow hit rocks.

✝ May 30

My day began under the half pearl of moon. At 4:00 A.M. I began to prepare a breakfast for Brad and me and put the plants out of the greenhouse. Breakfasted and chores done by 6:00 A.M., we walked over the mountain to keep our 6:30 A.M. appointment with the Johnsons to string fence. We were exchanging a work day for a work day: we would help them fence pasture today, they would help me skid my logs.

The cow had to be milked before Will could fence. I volunteered to help. Will professionally pulled the poor cow's swollen teats and sent hard streams of milk into the silver pail. I tried and got a dribble out of her, then a sizeable flow all over Will's pantleg. The method he showed me was simple, though I could not master the thumb-and-forefinger technique well enough to send pure white streams of milk coiling into the bucket. We carried buckets full of rich creamy milk into the house, where Dorothy separated it into various containers to make dairy products for her family.

Brad and I hung onto the back of Will's tractor as we bumped over creeks and rocky hillsides to the pasture needing to be fenced. All the Johnson boys came too. I was the only female in the crowd and was sentenced to lesser jobs of constructing rock jacks and stretching fence.

Brandon and I took the tractor up on the hill to gather rocks. Under one rock I discovered a hornets' nest, under another, two black beetles sparring in a corner. I wanted to sit and observe this natural phenomenon, but Brandon was revving the tractor up, and chores, it seems, come before enjoying the pleasures of the land which you work on.

By 9 A.M., the sun pounding on my back yelled, "Take your shirt off, Yvonne," but being the only female in a group of Mormon men, I was made to suffer like a caged animal, sweltering in my shirt. Of course, it was only natural that the men took off their shirts, which made me even hotter. My energy seemed of little significance when the men began to pound posts into the ground, my muscles being inferior in comparison to theirs. I walked through the pasture, balanced my way across Fir Creek, and went to help Dorothy with her tasks.

I cleaned up her yard for her, cleaned her house, folded laundry, and helped prepare lunch. I envied the men for being able to work in the fields and regretted being domestic and catering to the men. When they came in for lunch, Dorothy and I served them before we sat down to eat.

At 4:00 P.M. we were done, and Dorothy and Will thanked Brad and me for all the work they had gotten out of us. Around the first corner, out of sight from their cabin, I took off my shirt. Back at the cabin there were more chores to do—put away and water the plants, split wood, cook supper, bake bread, do dishes, etc. I fell asleep right after eating.

✚ June 1, 1975

I have seen an entire month change this land. The early May snows have all melted from the meadows and forest, where green grass now offers a setting for multicolored spring flowers. With 80-degree weather and sun the past two days, my skin is turning brown.

Yesterday at 7:00 A.M., the grinding sound of metal greeted me on my way up to the mountain. Will and his sons had come to help me drag my logs with their tractor. I learned quickly how to set choke and snake logs from the hillside.

The sun directly overhead, I went to prepare lunch for the men. They kept on skidding. My dishes were pieces of pine bark, which I lined with cheeses, fruit, and slices of my homemade bread. In the center of my fern tablecloth, I put a jar of peanut butter and one of honey, along with a freshly pulled bucket of creek water. Lunch over, I cleaned up the remains and went back to snaking logs. After a ten-hour workday and 75 logs skidded to the building site, the men and I rode down the hill on the tractor. Will would not even let me pay him for the gasoline he used.

Back at our cabin, Brad and I plunged our grimy, sweaty selves into the icy creek to suds away our accumulation of work. We emerged clean and pink, grabbed a whiskey bottle and headed down for the Doc's.

We spent a rather long evening drinking whiskey with the Doc. We all became fairly polluted, and the Doc drove Brad and me home. Brad regressed into an intoxicated six-year-old and pissed me off with his childish antics until he passed out in bed.

Rising this morning, I was very hung over. I again had had only four hours of sleep. Brad did not get out of bed all day. He was very hung over. I became annoyed with Brad today. His life style violently contradicts mine at times, and this of course goes two ways.

While he was sleeping today, I made a campsite for me on my land just below the building site. I have a soft grass-carpeted meadow bordered by an ancient uprooted ponderosa pine that separates my meadow from the forest. The area is lined with majestic tamarack, and the creek flows fifteen feet below where the tent will be pitched. Orchids speckle the grass all around.

I removed some rotten trees from my new home site. One of the trunks broke off, and out cascaded a stream of ants. They scurried to move an endless hoard of larvae. They would pick up an egg, move it a few inches, drop it, and retrieve another, never making any visible progress. I was reminded of city sites at rush hour. I picked up more logs and turned over more rocks to discover six different varieties of these six-legged, segmented creatures. Their sizes ranged from microscopic, almost, to an inch in length. The smaller ants usually are pale brown, with an exception of one category of red. The big ones are black and have three charcoal gray rings around their thorax.

I am hot and sweaty and take a quick bath, then rock on the balls of my feet beside the creek, thinking about the animal characteristics I have acquired since coming to this land.

No more nylons or bra straps, no quick lunch at McDonald's. I am a deer in the forest, sleek and brown. I fall asleep, naked, in the grass, but am chilled awake to the blue sky obliterated by a storm's gray overtones.

I walk down the mountain, and the incoming atmospheric turbulence engulfs the trees in an ocean of sound. I am startled by a three-eyed frog jumping from a spot of moss. As I bend down to examine closer this three-eyed amphibian, it blinks at me with its Cyclops eye and hops out of sight. Then a lizard slithers across my path so fast I catch only a darting glimpse.

Thunder, muffled by distance, rolls in with dark billowing clouds behind me. The wind is mysterious. A bat with bent radar flits over my head like a jerky marionette. I am glad when it flies into a pine tree. Two cones fall to the ground from its impact. The forest flushes out its creatures in advance of the storm.

Lightning begins. My strides quicken with the thought of being struck or crushed beneath a tree. A tan boulder in the pathway attracts my attention. It is not a rock but a young deer standing frozen, eyes and ears alert, only one hundred feet in clear sight of me. We have a stare-down for minutes, then, alarmed, she heads for cover.

Remorse fills me when I think that all these animals will be driven back into the woods this summer with the onslaught of visiting friends. I feel selfish for wanting this all to myself. The wind whips trees to and fro, hard. The needles make a raspy sound. I want to be tied to the tip of one of these trees and experience the life of a pine needle.

✝ June 2

From the outhouse this morning, I watched two deer graze on the hillside. They remained there, unaware of my watchful eye, until I tried to get a closer view. At the snap of a branch beneath my stalking feet they bounded off.

Dale came today, and we squared off the foundation corners. This type of work is above my head—angles, measurements, dimensions. Even though Dale patiently explained the process to me, I still don't exactly understand how to get a square corner. We built tripods to hold the corner strings straight and plumbed the pier centers.

Brad is irritating me more every day. Every time I watch him eat spoonfuls of peanut butter and wash it down with gulps of honey, I feel like wringing his neck. I cannot afford to feed him; he eats nine-tenths of everything I buy.

✝ June 3

My vanity is in a whirlwind. I sliced a six-inch gash on my face with a falling branch. We continued to square the foundation today. The site looks like an excavation area for an archaeology dig.

✝ June 4

Two blades of grass compete in a duel. The red sunset complements their tender green. I watched this picturesque scene from the white outhouse seat. I never beheld this type of entertainment from the wallpaper of city bathrooms.

It was pier-digging day at the excavation site. Shovel, pick, hand-made tamper, nine-pound sledge, and a ¾-inch piece of rebar aided the digging and squaring of the pier holes.

In my naivete, I assumed all sixteen piers could be measured and dug in one workday. I did not think ahead to the layers of rock below the surface soil. Brad showed me how to square a pier hole with a flat-faced shovel. I swore and threw the shovel when my first efforts ruined the precision of the hole. Then I sat calmly on a log, contemplated my mistake, and began again. I dug two forms perfectly. The holes are 13″ x 19″ across, and 2′ deep.

I got dirtier today than any other workday. When I clung to the creek's bottom, my bathtub, my shoulder was swiped by a miniature submarine. I caught a glimpse of red and blue and knew it was a rainbow trout.

✝ June 5

Too many unspoken words sour the sunset. Jean and Tony arrived this afternoon. I had been in town all day, but walking

up the mountain I felt her presence. At the old cabin there was a tiny kitten inside, gray and white, waiting on a chair. This affirmed Jean's return. I picked up the kitten and trudged up the hill to find Jean. The kitten got tired of being carried, so I put him down, and he followed me with his tiny feet up the mountain.

I met Tony on my land, and we exchanged a few shallow words. I felt uneasy around him. He said Jean went down the mountain to look for me. Four miniature feet followed me back down.

I am singing "Clouds" when I glance up to see Jean on the path in front of me, naked as I from the waist up. I had fantasized many hours before about what our reunion would be like. We approach one another, exchange a quick "hello," she drops her parcels, and we embrace, warm and sweaty. We hold onto each other tightly and cry until the kitten tries to climb up between our bodies. We break our embrace to include the kitten Jean has named "Cloud" and has given to me for a birthday present.

I ask Jean why she cries, and she says, "I feel lost." She cannot tell me why. I do not feel now the adhesiveness with her as before. We are close in the present bodily ways, but mountains apart in feeling. I ask her to come down to the cabin so we can talk, but she is too tired and must go set up a camp with Tony so they can sleep.

She has just come from the cabin and taken my down sleeping bag, after replacing it with hers; she needs the left one of the two in order to zip her bag together with the one Tony just bought. I want to lash out at her and call her a fucker. I feel stabbed again and hold the kitten tightly as I squat in the pathway, sobbing. She turns around and walks up the path. I walk back to the cabin, telling myself, "I refuse to be hurt by her anymore." Relationships are only a perpetual soap opera.

✝ June 6

My home now is a light bulb in the night. I moved into my tent today and have a new Coleman lantern for light. By its glow I can watch a variety of spiders climb the rip-stop nylon. I renamed Cloud, Tamarack, and he cuddles inside my sleeping bag with me. Once in a while the creek lets loose a boulder and interrupts the constant flow of its sound.

Jean is making it hard for me. Why? What have I done? She acts as if I stink, and is afraid to come near me lest she fill her nostrils with an essence not desirable. I'm the same person I was with her last year when we were in the throes of being passionate and dedicated lovers. No, I'm not the same person I was. I'm stronger this year, more sure of myself, and not as naive in how I relate with people—Jean especially.

Maybe that's Jean's problem, why she walks around me with an upturned nose: I don't smell the way she wants me to for her. So she finds what will suit her in a man who will play those giving games with her. I think Jean is jealous of me for what I have, who I am, and she is angry I cannot give this to her.

When I look at Jean now, it is as if I see someone I haven't seen before. I see a deceitful woman. That reflection mars the beauty I once only could see and turns my feelings for her sour. I'm thankful I am not living with her anymore, but wonder if it will be any easier living on the same land with her around.

✛ June 7

Swollen eyes. The handkerchief still wet from tears is wadded under my cheek. My nose is plugged from abused mucous membranes. No ambition to get up today. I just want to sleep away this self-inflicted pain.

Jean visited me late last night, woke me from sleep. We exchanged painful words and dying caresses. She left me in emotional upheaval. The contentment I felt inside myself before Jean's arrival has been replaced with constant grief and dissatisfaction since she returned. In the two days she has been here I have felt cold, hard, ugly. I just want to run away. Am I so immature in the subject of love I cannot handle my emotions? Can I not harden my feelings to block this pain from myself?

Because of my crying marathon last night, Brad sensed through my swollen eyes that something is difficult between Jean and me. He didn't ask, and I didn't tell him. I can't explain what is not clear to understand. I was bitchy to Brad most of the morning and apologized as we drawknifed trees.

I never gave it much thought before, but I now control the days of two men. Both Brad and Dale are working for me, and I like it when they call me "boss" and ask for affirmation before a decision is made. All of my life I have been a leader, and this situation now does nothing to tone down my domineering traits.

Orders given for the day, Brad and I set out to fill them: four post holes to be measured and dug. The work hard, tempers rise with the intensity of the sun. I've considered abandoning this cabin dream and leading the stereotyped life of a carefree teenager. Foundations, though, I am learning, are the anchors of dreams. Until a dream is secured to the ground, it is only a lofty ideal.

It seems since my arrival in Pine Valley I've spent ninety

percent of my time with a pack strapped to my back, hauling this and that over hill and dale. This evening I moved some of my belongings from the cabin up to my new tenthouse. I stored my clothes in two garbage bags; one holds work clothes, the other, going-to-town duds. Drawing materials and books are stored in the dented trunk that took a tumble over the Big Horn mountainside. What food I keep here is put in a bucket filled with rocks and sunk into the creek. I devised a small nightstand out of an old crate to hold my books and toiletries and the Coleman. In my cozy little home I have no noisy neighbors or rent due on the first of every month.

Soft and innocent, Tamarack shares my lap with a notebook beside the campfire tonight. Tamarack is adjusting to this life well and is filling my need for companionship. He follows me wherever I go. Walking up and down mountains, he has to take giant steps to hurdle obstructing logs and branches.

✛ June 10

On Sunday, I fasted and took an hour-long sweat. My body has never been in such fine shape—hard-muscled and brown from work. My deer fantasy is materializing into my flesh.

Mark came, and we went into town. It was '62 Days, the town's annual celebration of the old mining days. Mark bought beer and whiskey, and we drank and got drunk and watched a staged medicine show, complete with Indians wearing ceremonial Levis and surfer shirts.

I wore shorts and a rose-colored halter top and received whistles, compliments, and some lewd phrases. Mark, being the All-American Cowboy today and big brother protecting little sister, would give every one of these rude men a mean look or the finger.

We were pretty intoxicated by the time we left to drive to Mark's camp, which is more organized, it seems, than his state of mind. We climbed to a huge rock projecting from the rolling Blue Mountain foothills. Tamarack followed us up steep slopes of juniper and sage. The sunset permeated the sky with orange and put a feeling inside me that made my chest swell in the day's last rays.

66

On the way down, a swaggering porcupine crossed our path. Too slow to run from us, it curled in a corner of rocks to protect itself. Tamarack was very curious about this four-legged creature, and I grabbed him before his investigation became dangerously intimate. Porky's quills would bristle and protrude at the sound of our voices, expanding and contracting like gills on a fish. Mark threw a pebble at its back, and the quills stiffened on the ball-like form it puffed itself into, and slid from the pissed-off porcupine.

In town the next day I haggled with the merchantmen. I'm getting tired of playing their games, of the way they treat me. I bought forty bags of pre-mix cement at Mountain View Building Supply, and Pixie Creek Mill took my order for floorboards and rafters. Then Dale, who had driven me to the stores, and I went back to my land and mixed and poured enough cement to fill five pier holes.

✝ June 11

Those bags of pre-mix weigh only five pounds less than I do. My back is in agony from the day's lifting. After conjuring a lot of positive thinking and muscle, I was able to lift a 94-pound sack up into the wheelbarrow and let it fall with a relieving plop before I ripped it open and added the right amount of water to get a proper mixture, which was poured into the pier forms. If I had counted the endless push-pull motions of the hoe while sloshing cement to sloppy consistency, I imagine the count would have been in the ten thousands. Sometimes in mixing I would get careless, and the gray slush would slop over the wheelbarrow and onto my bare legs. When the piers are poured, they are finished with rounded edges by using my Girl Scout knife.

I cleaned all the tools good, then began on the job Brad had given up in frustration yesterday. I let loose behind the post-hole digger and crammed it through layers of rock to finish digging the other pier holes. Sometimes I had to use a sledge hammer to bust up rock. Brad sat on a log and just watched me; twice he told me to call it a day.

Sometimes I drive myself so hard that I think I will have a heart attack or nervous breakdown like my father. We both have similar foreheads and a work-mania attitude. Because of his drive, I am able to drive myself working on this cabin. His goal in life was to make enough money to give his children everything he never had as a poor boy. Well, he made his goal, but his kids lost their father when he died from a heart attack, stemming from the nervous breakdowns he was hospitalized with. Maybe someday I will learn to lessen my drive before it does me in.

A hardness has overcome me whenever I am around Tony and Jean. I avoid them whenever possible and on chance meetings keep my words short. My shortness is rubbing off onto Brad, especially since he is taking up with both of them in a very friendly way—they are becoming a nice threesome. But it is difficult to skirt around the concrete fact that we all live on the same land and share the same road to get to our respective camps. Jean and Tony have parked the jeep right below my building site. I watch them sometimes when I am building. It is strange to see Jean make the same moves with a man that we once made together—and had planned to continue making together.

Jean and Tony share a camp, a tent, and my sleeping bag in a meadow a distance above the end of the road, past the building site. Brad has a tent set up farther down from Jean and Tony, beside the creek. Brad and I set up a kitchen there, still cooking and sharing meals together. Then down the line is the building site and farther down the road is my camp, lying just inside my fence line.

I write this, down in my camp below everyone's, at the foot of my land. Alone here, I experience my greatest amount of contentment. I wonder if I'm unable to get along with people or just these particular people. I know I am hard to get along with, but will removing myself from people help me? Solitude will let me see clear.

✛ June 12

Slivers in my ass, creosote burns on my forearms, leg serrated by a clip of the bow saw. The day's work was slow. We spent the day hauling tamarack posts to the building site. I slapped creosote on the bottoms with an improvised paint brush I made from my old t-shirt tied around a stick.

Because it was so hot, I wore no clothes and got my butt full of slivers from the logs I sat on to slop with creosote. Rubbing my prickly bottom with one hand, I applied the dank mixture of creosote and kerosene with the other, dripping it all over my bare skin. Tonight as I write, I am painfully reminded that in the future I should wash creosote off my skin, pronto.

I am also, to my dismay, the owner of a deep, dark-with-blood gash on the mushy part of my calf. I was sawing with the bow saw, and it got pinched between the tree, then flew back and into my leg. I make another memo tonight: don't touch open wounds with creosote-covered hands.

After I cut myself, I had to go up to Jean and Tony's camp to get the first-aid kit. She saw me search the kit from where she was gardening, turned her back, and continued to hoe. Now my pain is more than physical.

Tonight at the campfire, Tamarack gnawed on some freshly decapitated mice he had caught. I watched him snap and pull on tiny mouse bones with his ten-week-old teeth. Every time a bone crunched, my stomach turned.

Jay Ellen and Ann (my sister) arrived this evening. They drove up in Ann's truck while I was working in the cabin. I gave a big hoot from the cabin foundation, ran down the hill, and embraced them both tightly, absorbing them into my dusty chest.

Ann, the baby of the family, my little sister, the unfortunate recipient of too many sibling jokes. She is my chubby counterpart, my bigger little sister. She is big boned and a couple inches taller than me.

Ann and Jay Ellen have driven from Minnesota to visit me for a while. Tonight beside a campfire we exchanged news. I revealed my dilemma with Tony and Jean. Jay Ellen is the first person I have aired myself to over this heart-throb issue. I hadn't known the affair had been bothering me so much until I felt the relief after my heart was aired out. I guess I needed to share this with someone.

✝ June 16

I drink my morning coffee, mesmerized by the maze of spider webs draping the trees, refracting the morning light onto the forest floor.

Another run-in with Tony and Jean yesterday. They accused me of stealing Jean's sharpening file. I was hurt and angry, became sick to my stomach, and walked away without even remarking on their cruel insinuation. I don't know what they're trying to do to me, but their hostility is real. I can pinpoint it coming straight towards me, though I can't understand why I merit the position of target.

Every day here with them becomes a challenge for me to get through. I feel a continual hurt because Jean and I no longer share a love that once was a part of me. It is as if she has retracted that part of her life from me, taken that nourishment with no warning, ripped it out of my heart made soft with love and replaced it with rusty metal shards that cut when I move and fester because of their tarnished nature.

I try to deal with the pain of my loss and turmoil by suppressing it. When I am alone with the sunset, the satisfaction I once felt is now shattered by my emotional uneasiness. My stomach is always squeamish, and my skin has broken out from all this worry and tension.

Fred Simpson came out today at my request to show Ann the other eighty acres below me that he wants to sell. They made an agreement over the price, so now my sister and I will be backwoods neighbors.

✝ June 17

Burned brush today. The flames got so high they licked branches on trees thirty to forty feet above. At twenty feet from the fire it was so hot it singed my eyebrows.

✝ June 18

Snow in them thar hills today intersperses with rain, and I worked a nine-hour day, getting frozen and drenched underneath the four layers of wool I wore for insulation.

70

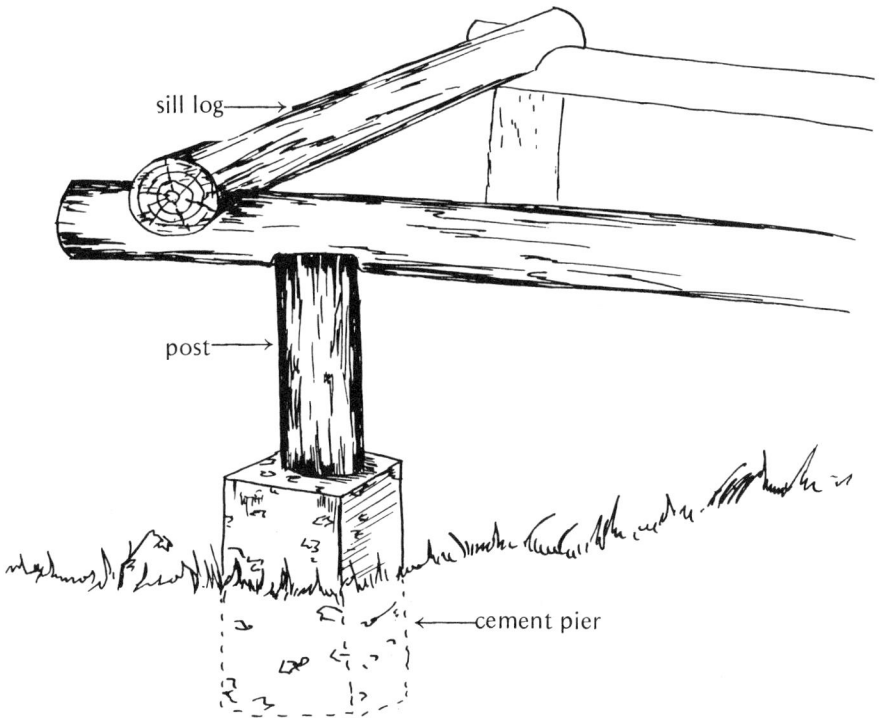

sill log

post

cement pier

We got the first sill log up today and fastened it down with rebar. I pounded it down in with Dale's eight-pound sledge hammer. I used a brace and bit for the first time today and drilled holes into the logs to pound rebar into, which will hold the log in place.

Dale showed me how to hew a log by scouring it with an axe. My first attempt, though determined, turned out rotten. I had Dale go over it, and rationalized my shoddy work by saying, "The first time I baked cookies, I burned them."

I ate a cup of peanut butter and honey mixed with raisins and cheese for lunch, hoping this high-powered mixture would keep me warm. When we quit at 5:30 P.M., I went down to my tent, which had leaked. I slept in a wet bag, not able to generate my own body heat to comfort.

✝ June 19

Rain falls as straight and plentiful as the pines growing upward. I walk the mountainside, wearing a beat-up old Stetson hat, stopping at whim to lick liquid diamonds from branches.

✝ June 20

The rains have stopped. Foliage washed clean. Went to town this morning and to Cathie's Cafe for fresh fritters. Jean and Tony were there. I said good-morning and took the only booth empty in the restaurant, behind them. It is bizarre to have no communication with this woman who was once half of me.

Brad and I hitchhiked to the lumber mill and were picked up by two cowboys driving a sprawling old Cadillac.

Back at camp, I take off all my clothes, lace up my moccasins, and run. Nebulous, naked and brown, I run and jump and kick sideways, laughing, with my hair being pushed in the winds. When I rest, I see a red-headed woodpecker inside a rotten tree. I creep up to it and discover it is stuck. He flutters in pain, his freed leg hanging out of the hole already broken. He pecks at my hand as I try to free him. I decide, after a long time of trying to dislodge the bird, the most humane thing is to kill him. Who am I, God, to decide his fate?

His last red-headed vision is of a gray stick crashing down. I scream as it hits his head. He flutters twice, and I moan. His slanty bird eyes roll gray and close, his head rolls to the side, he is dead and falls from the hole that had captured him.

I begin crying and rocking myself on the ground, looking down at the dead bird. This is the first living creature I ever killed. If it was stuck so tight when it was alive, how come it came loose when it died? Would it have lived if I had left it alone? I dig a grave and lay it in, its red-headed feathers the last I see before green and gray earth covers its body. I whisper, "I'm sorry." I walk home, sad, nebulous, naked—and a murderer.

72

✝ June 21

A full moon casts long gray shadows from tall pine and shrub in its light path. Roxy came from Minnesota on her motorcycle this evening. I greeted her arrival with mixed feelings. We sat close to the fire tonight, drinking spiced tea, sharing stories, the chill, and the moon.

Dale threw me in the creek today when I got too bossy with him; he just upped me over his shoulder and dropped me in the deepest pool. I held onto his pant loops, so he went with me. We spent the rest of the day laughing over this and working naked as our clothes dried on logs.

✝ June 22

Thirteen people came for a big lunch today. Jake delivered my stove all the way from Redmond. I bought a brand new chain saw in Butte City in the evening. The man who runs the saw shop, the mayor of Butte City, said, "Little girls like you shouldn't use chain saws." I replied, after I made sure he watched me practice buzzing logs in his front yard, "I've used bigger saws than this before."

✝ June 23

Lap-jointed all the floor joists in the sill logs today, using chain saw and chisel to make a mortise. I felt uneasy building with Brad and Dale. It was as if they had taken over all phases of this construction and just wanted me to sit and watch. Granted they know more than I, but if they don't show me what to do and let me work, how will I learn?

Had another run-in with Jean. This time she wants to take from me all the jars we had bought together. I got sick to my stomach and trembled with nerves. I don't know why she is being so hard to me. I have given her what she wants—her freedom and a place to live with Tony—but it seems this isn't enough. She wants my heart so she can kick it around.

Jean and Tony are spreading stories about me, some of which I don't even know how they can repeat, since what they say is based only on their personal vengeance. They tell people around here I am a dictator on this land. Well, shit!

What do they want me to be—the hostess with the mostess to them when they act spoiled? I think their way would be had if I were to leave this land to them, with a cabin on it so they could live in it together.

I feel alienated from Brad and Roxy, and sometimes even my own sister, because I refuse to banter or defend myself. If I could sue, it would be for slander. Only I do not know the reason they want to defile me before my friends. I guess if my friends are really my friends, they will see through the murk.

Dale took me home with him last evening. Sophie came to meet us on the path, running in her bare feet and bleached-by-the-sun overalls. Her eyes sparkled like ripe currants. We ate a supper by candlelight, candles hand-dipped by Chris from beeswax. Sophie and I drew pictures until she had to go to bed. We had deep conversations about Indian tipis, forest fairies, and frogs. A wave of loneliness passed through me when I watched Chris and Sophie hug goodnight. I love the child very much.

✠ June 24

Four wall logs up today and rebarred down, joists of 2x4s laid in. It still rains, making work slippery. I continue to eat cups of peanut butter and honey to keep warm. I work soaked and chilled to the bone all day.

✠ June 25

No one to make a schedule for me to follow, so I make my day to my self-satisfaction. Am I egotistical or narcissistic to enjoy my time alone here more than with other people on this mountain? Brad and Josie visited me at my camp last week and interrupted my reading. They said I reminded them of Thoreau. I share Thoreau's desire to be alone with my thoughts in the presence of nature, but I do not savor sharing Thoreau's thoughts. The man was a hypocrite; nor was he compatible with, nor could he enjoy, the world of people.

I wonder if I am not using this solitude and writing as a barricade against not dealing with a self-centered, selfish attitude inside of me.

74

The nineteen years of my life so far have been centered around others as well as myself. I have learned from others my faults and good qualities. Others have shown me my weaknesses and strengths. Others have nourished me, watered me with praise needed for my growth. I now choose to weave my own web, to feed myself praise and criticism. With my own nurturance, will I grow whole or weak? This is a test no educational system can offer me. No credits are received at the end of the course; the course is through when change has occurred, the credits, displayed in one's personality.

Not a busy day. After a long, contemplative breakfast, walked down to Will's to tell him his cows got through the fence and were heading onto my land. On the walk back home, I sang an improvised song about a free woman. With all my senses I sang. I found an obsidian arrowhead and an eagle feather and carried my treasures proudly as I walked home.

I had to fix the gate and toted along my fence-fixing pliers. I struggled with barbed wire for half an hour, trying to stretch new strands between the gate posts. I scared away the cows trying to get through by leading them in a rousing round of the national anthem, the eagle feather used as a baton.

✝ June 26

I have begun to accept my preference for women without putting myself through obstacles of persecution, self-hate, "how-weird-I'm-so-weird" complexes. I am a woman who enjoys loving women—as simple as that. Tonight I can utter the phrase "as simple as that" because in my solitude I am not put on audition in front of society's mores.

I reflect on the love Jean and I once shared. My coffee cup lets out wisps of steam into my homesick expression. Love . . . Am I too young to understand it? Will I ever? Too immature to have the strength needed to scale the heart's ramparts? Love . . . How can it be that the love two women once shared is being decayed into stench? It is because we are women with different needs. We are women playing games only women play, like cats.

Brad slips on the plastic sheets we use to cover the newly

laid floor. He impales his knee into his groin. Contorted in pain, he moans and grimaces. He is really suffering. I don't know what to do for him, so stand and offer what verbal comfort I can. I follow him as he hobbles back to his camp. I make him tea, do what I can for him so he won't have to move much. Tamarack and I then go home. He plays behind me until the grasses become too wet and high and I must carry him.

✚ June 28

> "I don't know where we went wrong, but the feeling's gone, and I just can't get it back."   —Gordon Lightfoot

The mountain closet queens live again. Jean and I decided to backpack up the creek and spend a couple days together, sorting through our rot. Our dwelling for this time is a natural rock cave. We unroll our sleeping bags on the most level, rockless area we can find. That first night we explore each other with uncertain passion. The love that once flowed between our compassionate bodies has dwindled and lies like embers. The next day we spend the warm sunlight hours on a hill, lying naked on our sleeping bags, trying to claim through touch the territory that I know, by intuition and the dissatisfaction of my fingertips and skin, will never be claimed again.

✚ June 29

In the institution of higher learning they taught me of colors with names of cadmium yellow, cobalt blue, vermillion, and chartreuse. In the school of nature I teach myself the hues of broken-robin-eggshell blue, witch-hair-moss black, flutter-by-butterfly yellow, dried-elk-dropping gray, deer-antler off-white, mush-red mushroom.

The moth attracted by the lamp's intensity seeks the illumination and flies into the desired, is trapped and burned to death. We, as people, are like moths in discovery: some survive the intensity; others become trapped and burn in curiosity. So much in every one of us are the moth and the fire.

✛ June 30

"Well, it's hard to be friends
when it was so easy to be lovers..."
—Rita Coolidge

These lyrics run through my head in the morning where I lie stiff and solemn in the sleeping bag beside Jean. This is to be the last morning of our two-day quest to unearth answers and alternatives to the way we treat each other. We have talked about our love, how it still exists but can't continue in the form we once shared. How then can we make it easier on ourselves and the others on this land to accept these changes? I experience pain in torrents from knowing the relationship will never be. Is it self-pity that makes me hurt so?

✛ July 2, 1975

Building this cabin is an infinite cycle of tasks. No sooner have I completed one step and think maybe there will be time for a breather than another phase springs out of necessity, and I am swamped in filling the needs of construction instead of my needs and the others' on this land. My mind is scattered by this onrush of work, whirling in ideas, plans, and tasks.

I've encountered a new difficulty in building—male dominancy. Brad and Dale, because they have years of carpentry experience, can excel in areas that I flounder in because of my inexperience. It has gotten to the point where they don't want to wait for me to learn by trial and error; they confer

with each other about what needs to be done, then do it, neglecting me.

The last two days, Brad and Dale have been doing all the notching. I have stood back and occupied myself with construction trivia because it takes me so long to notch. This evening I told Brad about my intentions to notch wall logs in the future. He said, "That will sure slow us down." Hurt and hot with anger, I replied, "How am I going to learn if you don't let me try?" This is my sandbox. I supply the toys and am supposed to sit back and watch the boys play.

Every time I went to nail a floorboard down today, Brad would race me to the spot and nail before I had the chance. I had to get damn obstinate about their letting me work, but my determination got me what I wanted and where I wanted to go. By this evening I was laying, clamping, and nailing down floorboards by myself. Dale and Brad stood back and watched.

At Hampstead's mill, my 2″ x 8″ planed floorboards were ready. Sam Hampstead, the owner, helped me load. The forty-four years he has operated a mill showed on his rough hands; I noticed a stump where a thumb should be. My inquisitiveness overpowered my good manners; thinking that his thumb was sawed off in his mill, I asked him just that. He answered, "Yes, I sawed it off in this here saw," pointing behind him to a huge circular saw in an old plank sawshed.

I picked up the insulation and also got that layed in. What a hellish, prickly job. Fiberglas, like malicious fairy dust, makes my skin itch. Put tar paper over this and nailed down some more boards. In all, I put in a fourteen-hour workday. No wonder I need to drink coffee to keep me awake to record the day's events at night, when the outer life simmers down to allow the inner life to digest.

✛ July 3

I'm so exhausted my body trembles from lack of sleep. I persist and drink coffee, which helps me extend my perceptions into the night. I have had four hours of sleep again. This strenuous work life and lack of sleep are taking a toll on my body. I cannot slow down. I begin to see self-destructive qualities in me. Most people I know put sleep and food as priorities in their lives; this gives a base for their light-hearted personalities and pretty fresh faces. My three to five hours of sleep a night, sporadic eating habits, and overconsumption of coffee leave me gray and hard like the rocks at Taylors Falls. But looking back, I can remember these moods and trouble sleeping even at three.

Jerry Porter, a high school psychology teacher, told the class about schizophrenics in their more chronic states of schizophrenia who would not sleep and would perpetually be planning or completing plans. If this is true of schizophrenics, then I have been one for at least the past eight months. Never before have I slept so little and done so much. Some mornings it seems I wake before falling asleep. My mind is always an endless motion picture of plans and ideas.

I have been told to slow down by many people. My intensity forbids it. Perhaps I should ease up a bit before my brakes give out and I am headed down a steep mountain road, alone, uncontrolled.

Rose with the sun and was in Butte City before anything was open, when the town cast an atmosphere of desertion. Hauled up the last of the floorboards. The main floor was finished today. I dance and leap over the planed pine-plank surface

✝ July 4

In dirty t-shirt I go to bed, too tired to care, and the Coleman lantern is silenced black.

✝ July 8

We all pile into Ann's truck and drive to Bygone Lake for a refreshing plunge. On the beautiful ride to the lake, I drink an entire bottle of wine. By the time I crash through the lake's icy mirrored surface, I am polluted, hardly feel the hard impact of cold water. I swim without a break across the lake in my intoxicated state. Back on shore I help consume another bottle of wine, on the drive home, another. and at Ann's cabin, hours later, one last bottle of wine before I stumble out into her front yard and collapse from alcohol and exhaustion into my sleeping bag. I grab one eyeful of stars before I pass into unconscious sleep.

I awake hours later, at about 4:00 A.M., riddled by troubled dreams of Tony and Jean. The dreams are gray and of endless corridors I walk through where people try to grab me. I am very hung over and see that the clear sky I fell asleep under now has rolling over it thick gray comulus clouds that look like dirty whipped cream.

At 8:00 A.M. Mark wakes me. The day, so early, is very hot. I take off my clothes and we talk. Ann joins us, freshly awakened from her sleep. We are three blurry-eyed Pepins together, alone for a rare moment since my mother's death.

Frank Miller came up this afternoon in time for lunch.

Later I walk him around my land, show him the building site. He tries to seduce me when we are alone. I restrain from giving him a knee in the crotch. He can't seduce me, so instead he offers to buy me. Says he will provide me with tar paper, nails, roofing materials if I spend a night at his cabin with him.

✝ July 9

Like artists, builders also must keep the tools of their trade in top condition for quality performance. Instead of brushes and pens to clean, I now have tools to sharpen. I have always kept my art supplies meticulously cared for; so now with my tools. I spent the morning sharpening drawknives, axes, chisels, and the chain saw.

Brad and I were laying the final loft boards when we were overtaken by a sudden hail and rain storm. We could not cover the floor with visquain quick enough, and water soaked the floorboards. A note to builders: always lay your roof before the floor.

It is late at night inside my tent. Tamarack annoys me by batting my pen as I write. A black ant has bitten my abdomen. My emotions are scrambled. I have heard through others on this land that Tony and Jean are planning to leave. I'm glad. It will leave me with a more peaceful life.

Any love I think there was left inside of me for Jean got sucked out of my heart as she continued to suck on my generosity, openness—and naïvete, which is why I was generous and open with her—I am still young and dumb in affairs of the heart. It's hard to imagine the change that can take place between two people in 365 days. One year ago we were the most passionate of lovers; this year we still exist in the intensity of our relationship but in realms of opposition. Jean is the first in a long line of lovers to fall, like dominoes. I will keep playing.

✝ July 10

Brad went to Mark's to help square his foundation today. That left me alone to lay the porch floor. I remembered the tools Dale had used to cut and measure the boards with, so I gathered up saw, tape, square, planer, rasp, pincher bar, hammer and nails. It was hard to haul the porch boards up onto the joists. I succeeded after great muscle-straining in the hot sun. I wore cut-offs and tennis shoes only, and the sun fried my skin.

When the boards were up, I began marking, measuring, and sawing, using my thumb as a guide the way I had seen Dale do. The perpetual motion of saw metal in pine plank caused me to work up such a sweat under the searing sun that my eyes stung from dripping perspiration. I have never worked up such a sweat before. Drops would splash on the boards I layed and roll into my eyes, stinging with their salt. I got three-quarters of the porch floor layed before I quit from the day's heat. I felt proud of my accomplishment; tapping into my own resources and not working to compete with anyone, I worked at my own pace.

I took the chain saw out into the woods to cut poles for a ladder. I had left my shorts hanging on the porch after washing away my sweat in the stream. I wore only my sandals to saw in. Chips of wood flew from the bar and were snuggled into my pubic patch, sawdust coated my chest and nipples. Being as egotistical as I am, the thought of submitting a photo of myself in this nude, chain-saw-wielding fashion to the saw's manufacturer crossed my mind. I liked working alone today. I did not feel dominated but equal, with my own abilities and inabilities.

✛ July 11

Today, the cabin seemed too much like work. I was about as enthusiastic to begin on it as I was to stand up eight hours a day behind an assembly line when I worked in the toy factory.

I had to lie on my back in the dirt and sticks to hammer above my head pieces of plywood used to encase the cabin's underside. Particles of insulation fiber would fall into my eyes along with dirt, temporarily blinding me as I drove nails upward. The horrible part of this job was not the filth and fiberglas fiber, but nailing. My arms would quiver and fall to the ground like wet string as my muscles defied the law of gravity, having to push the heavy hammer with impact enough to drive a nail above my head while I lay on my back in the dirt. The air turned blue with slang. Brad said I would make an excellent construction worker.

In the evening I spent time at my camp and did some domestic duties I've neglected in the wake of construction responsibilities. I wrote this kinda, sorta poem.

The Woodwoman's Housewife Sonata

No soap operas
No dishwasher
No board to iron wrinkles on.
An axe
A shovel
I dry my clothes on twine
tied between two tamarack.

I do not scour my toilet
which is a fallen pine
across a hole in the forest.
My bathtub is a stream
with no ring to scrape away.
My bathroom tile is the
colored rock bed
below the rushy clear.

My carpets are of lush green moss,
My dishes of dull tin and shined clean
with natural Brillo,
a pine cone,
and soap is sand.
My dishes clean
reflect my image.

My furniture is from
the forest showcase
and matches the decor
of woodland breath.

✝ July 12

How can I see the surrounding beauty when I can't see the beauty in me? My only home is the husk around my soul.

This afternoon I went insane, could not distinguish real from unreal. I stared blankly much of the day.

Had another run-in with Tony today. I stayed calm in the presence of his obstinate insinuations stemming from his insecurity at living on my land with the woman I once lived with. He takes childish forms to show his insecurities. After he left I was in a fury.

The whole thing with Jean and Tony seems like a squabble between some jealous second-graders. I have what they want and I won't give it to them, so they try to make things as difficult for me as possible, telling the other children that I am rotten so I won't have any support and they will. The only difference between our situation now and a second-grade classroom is that there is no teacher to help reconcile differences.

I talked to Brad about this recent confrontation. I told him about Jean and me being lovers and cried. He neither said nor did anything to console me. He probably wouldn't have consoled me anyway. Who would want to walk inside an internal combustion machine churning at full force?

My emotional intake and outburst caused me quite a headache. I could not relate to anyone all day, myself included. It was as though everyone was checking me on my faults. There was no neutral territory to escape into. How am I to live in this negative feedback? Am I as horrible as I feel to be to everyone? I felt as though he was about to yell at me for something all day. Where is one to go when there is no one to trust and no contentment inside one's own cave?

Brad told me a few days ago that Virginia Woolf, in a fit of emotional turmoil, flung herself into the night-colored waters of a river and drowned. Not that I feel like I'm Virginia Woolf, but the thought of ending my life, ending the storm inside me and finding peace, seemed very pleasurable. I thought of filling my pack, leaving this land to them, and thumbing my way, away. I wanted to breathe with and learn from other people. I wanted to see if I affected others as horribly as I seem to affect some people on this land.

> Self-destruct in the night
> late into
> one, two, three,
> the night.
>
> Ants crawl, black
> obsidian pearls in segments of three,
> they chew my leg, burrow in my eye sockets,
> they chew and pinch all my flesh.

Night claws rip through the tent
and shred me into strips
unclaimed by compassion.

The night has taken its toll.
The night, even the night,
will not take me.

The Coleman has fallen from its stand
and spills its iridescent white light
into blue flame that licks the tent floor,
my hair, into red tentacles of flame.

Tamarack, my faithful cat, has enlarged,
ten, twenty, forty times,
and drips the blood of his nightly catch,
shredded in compassionless shreds,
across my cheek.

I scream the silent words
of a mute heart, no one hears.

I self-destruct into the night,
one, two, three, I can count,
late into the night.

The ants have severed my feet,
carried them into the blackness—
in a blaze of blue, outside
the tent they lie, like
the heads of Medusa,
and wave their ragged
veins at me.

I have killed the cat,
strangled it with my brown, bony hands,
its neck snapped, crackled
like electric currents.

Something has snapped, inside
I scream and no one hears
the ocean which gathers me in voyage,

late into the night,
I self-destruct,
one, two, three,
late into the night.

Enamel coffins gnash in my mouth,
sending particles of fear flying,
covering the path, only I stumble.

✛ July 13

The Parkers, Mark, Brad, and I take a day hike to some
waterfalls near their home. It is a two-mile beautiful hike. I
find a brown duck egg in a stream. I carry Sophie on my back
and feel more comfortable than I have in weeks. The falls are
small, about twenty feet high inside a rock basin. The surrounding countryside—juniper, serpentine, openness—feels
sacred.

I feel a need to be alone and remove myself from the
others, splashing in the falls' pool. I sit on a rock overlooking
the first level of falling water. I am pulled into the tear-shaped
drops that fling themselves away from the bridal veil of falling water. These glass sculptures are so fine, yet they cannot
be purchased or made by the human hand. This is a creation
of nature that can be had only through the observing eye and
stored in the shelves of one's memory.

The land gives my mind room to run in. I sing songs that
express the turmoil I've been experiencing. The ancient juniper across from me harmonizes with my melancholy. Dale
comes to fetch me back to the group, preparing to leave. I am
startled like a deer, found out, and jerk out of my haunched
position. Walking back with the others, I feel lonely. Sophie
comes up to me and shivers from the cold. I open my shirt
and pull her inside me.

✝ July 14

Went to the doctor's in town today because of frequent bloody noses I've been having, plus having no period since I left Minnesota in April. I think these symptoms are a residue of my bout with Rocky Mountain spotted tick fever.

Dr. Pruitt, a young-looking man acting just like he has gotten out of marine training, is my attending physician. He shoves plastic tubes and his fingers inside my rose petal vagina. He pokes my ovaries, pushes down hard on my abdomen, and says, "Does this hurt?" I open my teeth that I've been gritting down hard and reply, "Yes." Through all my pain, he diagnoses nothing and writes out a prescription for progesterone tablets.

On the way back home I meet Tony and Jean on the path. She doesn't even stop her pace or look up when she trudges by quickly, saying, "We are hungry." It doesn't even hurt anymore.

✝ July 15

The green rip-stop nylon tent is alive with the muted sounds of frying fish. It has poured all day. I've stayed inside the limitations of my dwelling. There is only room to sit or lie down, but it is dry and protects me from the storm.

I am concerned over the cabin floor. Since the day it was laid, plank by plank, it has rained steadily, never allowing enough time for the boards to dry out. The rains have also delayed work progress.

The Coleman, primed and lit, illuminates the tent like a Chinese lantern in the night, and I sit, a fly attracted to bright intensity.

Throughout the day's rainy course, I have read Nigel Nicholson's account of his mother's diaries, *Portrait of a Marriage*. Vita Nicholson, prominent English socialite, writes about her love affair with another woman, Violet Keppel, and her acceptance of her sexuality.

I advance, therefore, the perfectly accepted theory that cases of dual personality do exist, in which the feminine and masculine elements alternately preponderate. I advance this in an imper-

88

sonal and scientific spirit, and claim that I am qualified to speak with the intimacy a professional scientist could acquire only after years of studying and indirect information because I have the object of study always to hand, in my own heart, and can gauge the exact truthfulness of what my own experience tells me. However frank, people would always keep back something. I can't keep back anything from myself.

This nineteenth-century woman, so honest and accepting of her sexuality, makes me more comfortable with mine.

+ July 18

Sharp, angry—much too angry—words surge. I went up to their camp to get the address of a mutual friend. They won't give it to me. They say I will write lies and mail them. Tony calls me a "fucker," Jean, a "spiteful little girl." I tell them to leave as quickly as possible. For my sanity, today is not soon enough. They have affected me like parasites, draining my will, my spirit. Love has turned to hate—this is the most terrible thing.

+ July 19

This is beyond the intensity of the nightmare I once only imagined, this reality I live in now. Back in Minneapolis, I would pessimistically conjure up the most negative of circumstances that could part Jean and me. I would imagine this to prepare myself for the unsavory event of our love's termination, to have in my mind already the experience of coping with this pain. But my negative assumptions then did not envision the degree of pain or that a loss of one's center could be this definite or lasting, taking such a toll on the structure of my contentment. It seems now everything we once shared in love has turned to the contrary, to tarnish.

A shroud of heaviness lifted from my chest after I told them to leave, although I am still troubled very much. I can sympathize with their position of exile, and I feel like the almighty ruler, high enough to designate who stays in my country, my land. I exercise my power for the health of the people on this land, and I consider my asking Tony and Jean to leave a healthy decision.

In the midst of drawknifing a ceiling beam today I was overcome with fatigue. I had to ask Brad to finish for me, then I called it a day. I don't know whether my bodily statement is physical or emotional, but ever since I started taking those progesterone tablets Dr. Pruitt gave me, my energy level has been zero. I told Brad of this, and he said, "They have made a woman out of you."

✝ July 20

Mark opens the flap of my tent and yells, "Howdy." Outside my tent, Ann is crashed out in her sleeping bag on the ground strewn with empty beer bottles and wine jugs. My mind is quickly circulating memories of a few hours before. Last night, Ann, Hal, her boyfriend, Brad, Roxy, and I all shared wine and talked around the campfire late, late into the night. Everyone became extremely inebriated except me. I have had three and a half hours of sleep.

They told me that they support my decision to tell Jean and Tony to leave. They say that they had seen through the lies. It is good to know who your friends are; they are friends because of how they pull through.

✝ July 21

That dirty pair of underwear has lain rumpled in the corner for a week now. The colored pencils, once arranged according to hue, now lie askew and stray from the pencil case. Some more clothing, a flashlight, and of course numerous books and paper add to the mess. I've had no time in the last week to be Suzy Homemaker. I have been too busy being Betty Builder. It makes me tired just to think about the Herculean jobs I carry through daily. I can never complete all I set out to do in a day. Sometimes the days are so full and busy that they never seem to have happened. Today, for example, was one of them.

I woke and shook a warm, sound sleep from my head at

6:00 this morning. Short rays were already cutting through dank morning pine. Face washed in the stream, wood split, fire made, coffee put on, Tamarack fed, I wrote an hour, then up to the building site, where we layed the rest of the loft floor for the next ten hours. I became angry trying to pound nails into the ends of boards at 45-degree angles. As the nails bent, I threw a tantrum, then my hammer, and sat in the corner and sulked.

Again it was a hot day. Brad and I worked naked except for sturdy work boots. When Dale came later in the morning, he also undressed. It is absurd; we wake in the morning and dress, then get to work and undress for work. The sight of three naked builders would put any building inspector in awe. I wonder if nudity is to code?

While Brad and I did the floor, Dale sawed out the windows and framed the door. Progress is really beginning to show on the cabin. At every eyeful I am amazed to think that the cabin was once only raw forest, standing, branched.

In the evening I walked down to the Doc's, who had said he would take me to Pixie Creek to pick up my rafters and roof boards. Brad came too; I had promised him ice cream. We all stopped for treats at the Prairie Maid. I bought a huge banana split for $1.09, ate it, then chased it with a large chocolate cone.

At Pixie Creek Mill, I pulled $34.44 from my wallet and handed it to shy Ken Holdman. This paid for half of my rafters. As of late I've been spending *mucho dinero* on cut lumber, but the expenditures justify themselves in revealing quality building. I like Ken Holdman a lot; he shines the image of a timid fly.

It is already dark on the drive home, and the moon illuminates the right side of our faces as we talk.

After unloading the boards, we give the Doc a grand tour of the cabin, cast in the eerie light of a full moon. Again I am amazed at this log structure that takes form in the night like an iridescent stockade. I walk to my camp, later, on a path patched with moonlight and Tamarack's white fur, which contrasts with the night.

✝ July 22

The only purpose for going to town today was to attend the doctor's appointment I made when I discovered the progesterone tablets that were supposed to make a woman out of me failed, in their overdose of hormones, to induce my menstrual cycle.

After a long wait I am let into a small, sterile room, told to remove my clothes, and draped in a starchy paper. Dr. Pendell, with his junior doctor intern, comes in and begins to poke his hand between my legs. Pendell reports to the young doctor on the contents of my uterus. Pendell pulls his hand out like he has just finished stuffing a chicken. He walks out of the room, saying to the junior doctor before I can protest, "Give her tummy and her small uterus a feel."

With the apprehension of a puppy punished for puddling on the floor, the young doctor presses my abdomen, then puts a clear plastic glove on the hand that he will meekly probe my vagina with. He looks as if he just got caught peeking at the girls in the high school locker room. Then his face captures the expression of "Oh, look what I'm doing," but an "Ish!" escapes as he pulls his vaseline-coated gloved fingers from me.

Dr. Pendell comes back into the room and says he cannot diagnose my problem and that I should go to the large hospital for a series of tests. When they leave the room, I wad the kleenex covering that I rip off my body and throw it in the corner—along with my respect for their practice of healing.

✝ July 23

Three segments of a jet black ant contrast with the pearly white of Monterey jack cheese. I watch an ant crawl flatly beneath the cellophane wrapping, printed with the cheese's name and price. I have my supper in the doorway of my tent —mixed raw nuts, a ripe nectarine, and the Monterey jack cheese, complete with ants. It is 9:00 P.M., and I have just returned from working thirteen and a half hours on the cabin.

Very early this morning I was chopping away a level surface on the windowsill sawed out yesterday when Brad bellowed, "Breakfast!" I dropped my silver cutting tools and headed across the creek to see a large black cast-iron skillet on coals, simmering with smells. I ate two large platefuls of Brad's morning concoction: lentils, rice, onions, and pineapple. Afterwards two cups of morning coffee with bird-song accompaniment. Brad and I have been communicating much better lately and have talked of plans to hitchhike together for a month after the cabin is finished. I am so thankful he entered my life.

I have discovered the tools that work for men haven't necessarily been made to be used by a woman. The reason it took me so long to notch a log before was because I was using a tool not made to be handled by me. Brad and Dale used an axe to notch; consequently, so did I. But the axe felt awkward, and I could not manipulate it with any degree of accuracy. When I was straddling a log, notching today, my axe fell down, and I had to resort to using the hatchet strapped onto my tool pouch. I found the smaller tool to be much more appropriate to my abilities. I did everything right today, and my notches fit together snug, the way Dale's do.

There are three primary steps to my method of notching.

1. Mark logs with wing dividers; draw the contour of the bottom log onto the upper log by keeping the divider tips at a 90-degree angle.

2. The log should have an oval marking. Fasten the log to be notched with a board, or log dog, onto the bottom log. Serrate the notch mark with the chain saw, always starting in the center and moving out, careful not to cut out your marks.

3. With a hatchet, chop out the wedges and finish your saddle with a chisel. You will have to roll the log over and refit once or several times.

Into the second notch of my afternoon, Dale yells for me to put my shirt on because I have visitors. Brad quickly throws me his, as my plaid shirt is down on the ground and to retrieve it I would be in full view of the visitors. Brad's shirt is the "V"-cut type and the "V" hangs down open to reveal both my breasts. Dale throws me his shirt, which is just as big, but buttons well enough for the public eye to view me without blushing red in embarrassment.

1. Place wing divider on top log, keeping point straight, trace diameter of log to be notched.

2. Use chain saw to cut notch. Starting in the middle, serrate the notch mark using cuts one inch apart.

3. Whack out serrations with hatchet. Use chisel to make a smooth, round finished notch.

After all this hurry-scurry, Sam Hampstead is right below the cabin and wants to know where to put my lumber. This huge-hearted, sixty-year-old man has delivered my lumber out of kindness. I give him a full tour of the cabin and have to tell him that I have helped build it too, because he thinks only Brad and Dale do the work and I watch. When Sam sees the chain saw, he begins to tell me bloody, gory stories about people with sliced faces and sawed-up legs. He says, "Be careful, kid." Even though I resent being called a kid, I reply kindly that I am very cautious. Lately, though, I've been sawing entirely nude save for my thick boots. This is risky, besides being risqué, and no matter how careful one can be, accidents do frequent the normal flow of events.

94

✝ July 24

Always tons to be done. Tons I want to do. To be a painter, a writer, a scholar, a carpenter, a nursery-school director, a pack-bearing vagabond. I am on my own, playing the wheel of fortune.

Back in the city, so many women are pushing for liberation. I have realized that liberation happens inside of me before it can honestly and securely hold the rest of the world. I have to have the strength to hold my world or else the rest is superficial, a ploy to make me think I'm strong and free. I know many feminists fighting for equality; but given equal opportunities, these women use their femininity as a fall back for not wanting to deal with the equality they have achieved. I know women who can profusely expose doctrine and theory about the women's movement, how we must continue to struggle to gain our strengths. But give them a pick or a shovel and tell them to use it, they will flatly refuse, saying they are not strong enough even before trying.

✝ July 25

Tamarack was a spiteful feline this morning, chewing on my fingers, batting my face and hair with his paws. I threw him out of the tent when the morning light was still gray with shadows before the sunrise. Tamarack did not like being excluded and climbed on the tent sides, crying, his claws piercing the nylon.

Everyone has gone out to dinner with Tony and Jean. I stay at camp. Ever since the day Tony and Jean arrived, my life has been a torture of jagged, emotional jumble. Despite the effects this constant trauma has had on my disposition, Brad and I have remained on good terms, though occasionally he has taken sides.

Sometimes I am possessed by waves of belligerence, nastiness, impatience, and other human foulness. I am not able to see clear of these moods for long uncomfortable hours. Brad, dressed in patience, has ridden out and held up under my emotional barrages that left him excluded in the iciness of my rejection. I cannot relate to another when I cannot relate to myself in good feeling.

Brad's congenial temperament has pushed me to reflect on the ugliness inside myself instead of finding blame to rest on the outside. I am left to see the negativism that develops and resides in me instead of being created by others and funneled into me. Brad has not supported me through my dilemma with Tony and Jean, but has been there watching as I floundered to find support in myself.

✢ July 27

> The night, well into its life,
> has the moon
> not full anymore
> but a cycle of light
> bright enough to drench
> a path to camp.
>
> There is a series of gates
> to open and shut
> before I reach home,
> the toll, a snag
> by barbed wire,
> and a curse paid
> to the snag of barbed wire.
>
> At the last gate, guarded by
> rose hip bushes,
> a probing segment of the pink prickle-
> bearing bush must be pushed
> to get to the ingress
> or outgress,
> depending.
>
> The last few ruts are
> scaled. I am entralled
> with night's territory,
> rich, dark, secret.
> A thought of the contrary
> saddens my heart.

Through the moon-captured night,
the last steps are taken.
I feel down the path
known by heart.

Every jag, jet and soft land
conquered, safely.
At camp, this is written
by candlelight.

✝ July 28

Laid the rafters on the roof today and started to gable both
ends with logs. The heat on the roof was unbearable; the only
thing keeping me from being baked through were frequent
plunges into the creek.

I awake with a jerk this morning to Jean outside my tent,
yelling my name. She has brought some mail for me with the
message that she and Tony are leaving today. I do not express any emotion, positive or negative. I give Jean a drawing
I've done of the two of us embracing, naked, on a mountain-
top with a vista of a valley below. I hand the drawing to her,
saying, "This is for the love we once knew." Jean glares at
me and says, "Keep it. It's in my head."

I feel swords of hurt shove up from my belly through my
heart, and I hold a tight rein on my emotions, as the slice of
pain will cause tears. I do not want to cry in front of Jean or
show that, unlike her, I may still feel a loving vulnerability.
Jean takes a book of hers, turns, and walks up the hill without saying anything—in a hurry, I imagine, to forget me.

I lie back down on my sleeping bag. Tamarack reclines on
my chest.

Later, in the meadow above the Doc's, on a patch of hillside rising higher than the surrounding hills, I sat smoking and
watching Jean leave down the same road we had come together on, three months ago, to build our new life. The jeep
was packed to the top, and at the Doc's they left the tipi
poles Jean and I had cut. I was discreet on my hillside with
the juniper. They never knew I was watching them and crying.
I watched them talk to the Doc for almost an hour, trying to

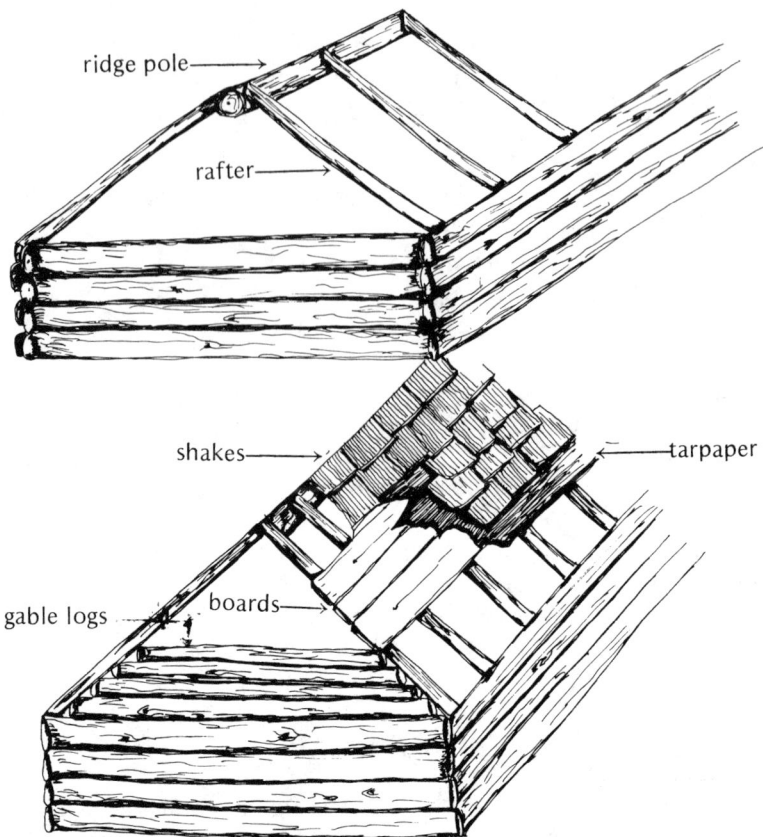

ridge pole

rafter

shakes

tarpaper

gable logs

boards

convince him, I imagine, that I was a horrible person for asking them to leave.

My perceptions seemed rinsed of the muddied emotions that had hindered my vision these past few months. I started to see things, sharp and clear. Bright orange patches of fungi on gray granite drew my eyes, a single daisy on the forest floor, resting in its solitary display of life beside some sun-bleached bones of a deer kill. In the decaying orange and reds of the day's setting, I felt positive; a new story was being woven into my organs, one of relief, of clarity. I had begun the process of washing myself clean of dark emotions.

In the meadow while watching Jean leave, I wrote a poem and read it to the yarrow bobbing in hot evening winds. The sound of my own voice cracked the shell I had tried to fortify through my feeling. Tears swelled and I let them spill, then be pushed by another onslaught releasing my anguish. The yarrow cried with me. I felt strong in the camaraderie of the mountains.

The last few steps to my camp were accompanied by a mule-tailed deer crossing my path and a goshawk that flew from the woods, directly over my head, lifting itself into the dusk-coated evening. The appearance of these two creatures I felt was some kind of omen. What does the combination of this life mean? Back at my camp I soothed my wound with a thick salve of supper, peanut butter and honey, and was appalled at the fragrance of cremated moths. In their greed they burned with the intensity of the lamp.

There is force
Desolate as pine needles.

The yarrow flower moves with solitary winds
and pine and me. Grasses that whisper
mahogany branches that clack, the creak of
an old pine, reflect sorrow of my aloneness.

On a hillside older than my sad soul,
I meditate on the nature and remnants
of a relationship that sickens and
hollows my heart.

Three dusty-dry tears.
I watch her leave on the same
road we once traveled together.

I am the only animal on this wind-
dancing hillside with tear-stained
cheeks, though like the juniper, pine,
and yarrow, I am the same. We blow
alone in aloneness with and against
the winds.

1. as far from myself
as I try to get
or think I have gotten
I always return
not having gotten far.

2. like fine blue silk
our love once was,
now tattered rags,
our remnants.

3. I let
the hurt and anger
out by writing and
drawing. I am hard
as what I create.

4. Sometimes I want
to be held and cared for,
the child inside
that never breathed.

5. We loved together
one year, one year,
not enough, maybe
too much.

6. some days I sing a lot
and smile and say to myself,
"Look at me, I'm happy,"
as though to verify an air
of inner contentment
I question now.

7. Enough of this sorrow,
picking the scab,
waiting for blood.

8. I will put on my
Wonder Woman cape and
slap on the Ol' American smile
and fly, away.

✛ July 29

Nothing, it seems, operates according to my plans, nothing. I was fed up today with all the cogs it takes to keep my wheels in motion. There have been more times in this day than not when I wanted to say, "To hell with it," leave, scream and cry and kick—in general, let out all those unsavory disappointments mounting to explode into a volcanic tantrum. But I will not let blow, my control suppressing it.

I bought an old green ¾-ton, 1962 Ford pick-up for $300 that needs a valve job and new muffler. I just bought myself more worries and complications.

✛ July 30

I oftentimes find that the hour of the day in which I write has, to varying degrees, an effect on articulation. For instance, at night when I write, I struggle to stay awake; thus the words splatter haphazardly over the page. Because of the hurried state of mind, trying to fight off a sleep that overpowers perceptions, my thoughts are not given considered expression. To write well, I should be fully rested. The intent of conveying my thoughts in a literary manner must be supported by the quality of my energies.

When I try to write in the afternoon, I am pulled by guilt, based on the neglecting of daily duties. Hours of light in these mountains are for sustaining one's life: chopping wood, cooking, fetching water, building—the perpetual advent of essential events that support one's comfort. The result of trying to write in the afternoon is again another slipshod display. There is really never any time for me in which to write with the proper balance of ease and tension, unless I religiously devote a section of the day to convey the word and stick to my schedule.

Constant chaos the day has been at Ann's cabin. Our sibling bond was given a chance to live again, forced together inside of Ann's cabin to wait out a thunderstorm.

I drink coffee in the loft and sketch Ann and Mark below, baking cookies and cooking soup. Mark stirs a pot of barley and black pea soup. Ann plops gobs of peanut butter, honey, oatmeal, and chocolate chips onto a cookie sheet. Fragrances fill the cabin. I eat a dozen cookies that Ann tosses up to me in the loft as she spatulas them off the cookie sheet. I am reminded of scenes from *The Snake Pit* as I watch my two siblings below compete for space at the wood cookstove. I comment how fortunate we are to own our own land and homes, being so young and still being able to take leisure and eat cookies. No response comes from them. Sometimes I think anything above the subjects of food and dope is too much for their comprehension.

The sketch I have done from the loft with colored pencils turns out not good, not bad. I exhibit it to Mark and Ann. They say, "It stinks." So much for constructive criticism. The rain has stopped by the time my critique is over with, and I can find no excuse not to remove myself from the loft and walk up the mountain to work except for my mood of lethargy created by the cabin's warm cooking smells and my belly bloated with cookies. So I just lie in the loft and eat cookies, laughing with my family.

I again bring up the topic of our privilege of owning land to arouse some legitimate conversation. This time they are receptive, and we all talk like English snobs, playfully. I am reminded of Bloomsbury; however, our abode does not resemble the culture and refinement of Virginia Woolf's house and family. In comparisons, the Pepins never dress for tea, or dinner for that matter, but wear the same pine-pitchy soiled clothes to dine in that they have worn for two or three days. Our parlor is the pine woods, and meals are simple soup and bread. We are carefree mountain dwellers, running the meadows and hills in dirty jeans and plaid shirts.

When Mark and Ann have finished cooking, they come up to the loft with me. The onyx bowl is filled and passed many times. We are very jovial and sing, whistle, laugh in unison. Our talk is so ridiculous our sides almost split from laughter.

This threesome is regressing into infantile mannerisms, but it is good; we laugh honestly. Our actions are so childish; we tease and jest each other. I treasure—we treasure this moment. The last five years for us have been piled high with misfortune and struggle—sadness that has separated us.

I remove myself from the loft to go below and write in my journal. From the green rocker where I sit, trying to concentrate, I hear whispering. Glancing above through the floorboards' crack in the loft, I distinguish two pink sluglike forms moving in the open slats. Before I realize the intent of the absurd position of these lips, a strand of spittle falls from them onto my leg. Those little pigs have spit on me and roll in the loft, convulsed with laughter.

Retaliation comes after my astonishment has worn off. Seconds later I grab the wooden spoon inside the bowl of cookie batter, and I catapult blobs of dough upward into the faces of my loving family. They scrape off what they can and throw it back at me. We have a full-scale war going. When the cookie ammunition is used up, I fill my spoon with barleybean soup and shoot it upwards. They again scrape from their faces the soup that has splattered over them and the walls, and fling it back down. Ann pours her only reserve of ammunition my way, a cup of coffee on my head. We are eighteen, nineteen, and twenty—or are we one, two, three years old? I take my leave, but first take the ladder away from the loft, where they are stranded in our loving mess.

✛ August 1, 1975

The spirit in which one writes creates one's written manner. I have no incentive to write this morning and do so unimaginatively, since moments spent alone with words are few and unlock meaning in the process I struggle through. When this cabin is finished being built, I wonder, with more time to write then, if the desire will still be there?

Later: Towards 6:00 P.M., I board my old green tank of a truck and drive to Prairie City to pick up roof boards. On the way, windows open, my hair blows through. I eat apples and wave at other truckers. Despite the undesirable condition of the truck, we were meant for each other.

103

At Hampstead's Mill, the normally short process of sorting and loading 1″ x 12″ roof boards is expanded into two hours, as Sam, the thumbless owner, likes to talk a lot. He tells me about growing up in Regina, Canada, on his father's homestead, and how his mother would freeze the tip of her nose just walking to the well for a bucket of water. How they would stretch chicken wire around the barn and fill the opening full of wheat chaff to insulate against the winter. Sometimes it got so cold his family would all crawl into the same bed. When Sam was eight years old, he got an earache and suffered so bad that his father hitched the horses to the sled and drove thirty-six miles in subzero weather to the doctor's.

Sam tells me that when he was eighteen, he hitchhiked to Butte City and began to work at a lumber mill, sawing wood for ninety cents an hour. He has scraped a living from the lumber industry for over forty years, raised five kids off what he took home. Sam has seen hard times I probably will never know. He talks now about the government—how taxes suck any profit he makes, how Social Security is cheating him of the money he fed into the system. His words are bitter and his eyes misty when he says, "In my sixty-one years I've never gotten ahead."

✝ August 4

The truck is loaded with 150 pounds of nails, some tongue-and-groove paneling, six sacks of cement, tar paper, half a yard of sand, and some groceries. I drive to mechanic Greg Anderson's corrugated-metal garage. The tank is being brought in for a diagnosis. Greg, a short but strong, stumpy man with a cherub face, quits work, and we go under my hood. He takes off the valve cover; I hold the valve gauge and get grease squirted in my eyes. I have a burnt valve. We put in new points and plugs, a few other minor things. He is amazed I get under the hood and learn by helping. He says, "My old lady would never do that." I hate it when people call their mate "old lady" or "old man." Anyway, sweat is streaming off both our faces in the afternoon heat. I wipe the grease off my hands, and we make a date to give the tank a valve job on Sunday. This seems odd to me. He picked the date, after saying he doesn't work on weekends.

✝ August 5

Was very sick today, though I papered the roof and insulated between the rafters. I felt so terrible all day, I had to quit work twice and lie down. Despite my illness, I mustered all my force to lift 120-pound rolls of mineral paper up onto the porch. I have never lifted anything this heavy before and think I overdid it, as there is a point in my vertebrae that hurts in a way I have never hurt before. It is an awful feeling to ache and be nauseous on a roof, absorbing the smell of tar paper.

Tonight I have a chill and shake so from it I can't bathe away the itchy insulation on my sweat-dried, sticky skin. My only wish now is that someone will come and massage the aches and chill out of me. Dale is coming tomorrow. I have to be well and free of this misery. Maybe my Wonder Woman role is vulnerable to the flu—or whatever misfortune has infiltrated me.

✝ August 6

Painful, endless—I rode the crest of this illness wave alone. After a horrible night when I dreamed I was lashed to the cabin rafter in a lightning storm, I rose parched with thirst but too weak to walk to the creek and procure water. When I stood up, my stomach turned in pain; I clenched it with my hands, and the forest began to spin in the light, airy currents of my head. I twirled backwards and landed halfway in and out of the tent, face down on the sleeping bag. I was very weak when I returned to semiconsciousness and still dry with thirst. I swam in and out of a pain-riddled sleep for two hours until Brad, concerned because I was not out pounding on the cabin at sunrise, came to check on me. He asked what he could do to help me. I said, "Just let me die in peace."

Long into the afternoon the stomach pain was so unbearable that the only remedy I could think of that was on hand was precisely that—on my hand! I'd read that when people overeat or drink, they could stick their finger down their throat to make them regurgitate. I went outside to try this, hoping to relieve the discomfort in my belly, but ended up only exhausted from the effort and the back of my throat

1.

2.

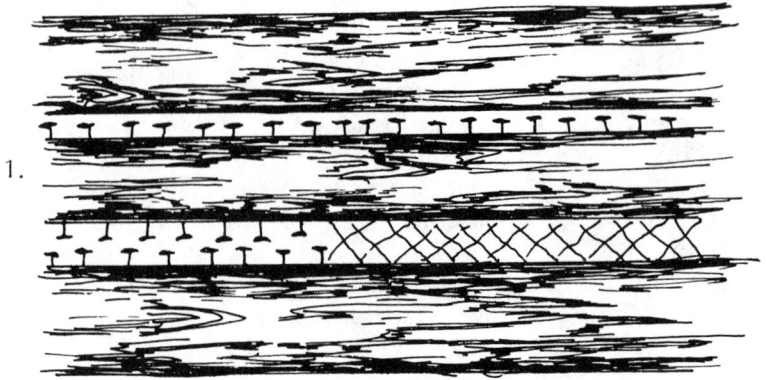

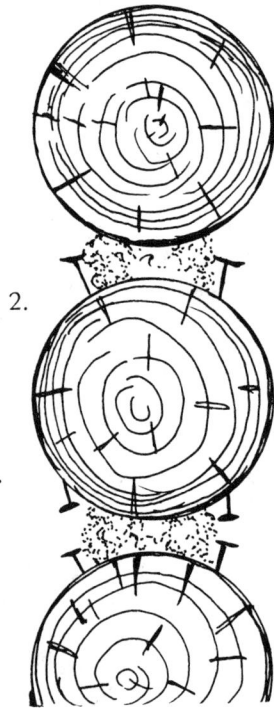

1. Use nails or chicken wire depending
   on width to be chinked to hold
   insulation in and hold mortar on wall.

2. After first side of nails or insulation
   is put in logs, stuff insulation from
   other side and finish with more nails
   so there is a cage effect.

106

bruised. Now I truly know what it is like to be alone. I understand with compassion what it must be like to be elderly and not able to care for your own needs. I slept the rest of my day, waking at sunset to cover myself.

✦ August 8

Brad and I try to cover the insulation with paneling, but I am still too weak to hold up the boards, so we revert to pounding eightpenny nails into the logs to secure the mortar when troweled between the cracks. We pound them in every log on both sides, about two inches apart, then bend them up in the crack. It is very monotonous work—boring, to be exact.

After two hours of this I again am very weak and walk back down to my camp to sleep. After nappy time, I work until after dark.

✦ August 9

A twig snaps in the distance. Glancing up from my morning orange campfire, I see a ten-point buck one hundred feet into the woods. As I write this down, two does and two more bucks flash the whites of their behinds in a startled thrust through the branch jungle, camouflaging their antlers amidst bare sticks.

The air holds an early morning chill, enough so that I wear long pants and two wool shirts. Summer seems to have retreated, allowing fall to come, prematurely. Summer was like a bud that didn't have a chance to flower, a sparkler that only fizzled. In the mornings I have to warm my clothes inside the sleeping bag, and rocks on the ground have frost on them, reminding me of a cheap breakfast cereal I used to eat as a kid.

The hawks have just woken up. I can hear their crying in the sky. A mother and three babies warn me with their shrill screeches every time I come up the road that this is their territory—something I fully acknowledge. I will do nothing to harm these living ornaments of the sky. Their presence is a gift.

Nails, eightpenny galvanized nails, hundreds, thousands, multitudes, galaxies of these little metal soldiers I bash into logs, one to two inches apart. Maybe not multitudes or galaxies but at least thirty-five pounds of nails I have pounded into the logs so far. In the evening I secure an elk antler on the newly hung cabin door with 16-penny nails, slamming them in with a 22-ounce waffle-faced hammer. No Paul or Pauline Bunyan could ever yank off my door handle.

Shadows fall long over the valley when I leave to drive the tank down the mountain to pick up some insulation. I have the engine rumbling, warming up, and I get out to remove the blocks I've placed under the rear wheels for added security, as the emergency brake is finicky. As soon as I've removed the second block, the truck starts to roll backwards, first creeping and then gradually increasing its speed downhill. I make a mad dive for the door handle that most always sticks shut, but luckily I have put a block of wood in the door and can yank it open. I pump pressure into the brakes to stop it— only a few feet from the embankment. I give a yell of relief and resume shaking in my sweat.

Back at the cabin after dark, with a full load of insulation, the headlights graze over the cabin's exterior. Walls all up, porch laid, roof on, windows and doors in. The cabin looks complete from the outside. "Charming" is an accurate adjective to describe it. So much work done, so much more to do.

✚ August 10

At the post office I receive a letter from Jean and fall on the floor reading it. The section contorting me in joy simply reads, "I have made many mistakes. I still love you and guess I always will."

Main Street, Pine Valley, Saturday night. The natives are out and looking for life. Neon slaps my face, my ears are pierced with the sound of country western music. I find myself cross-legged on the pavement underneath the red and blue stripes of the barber shop across the street from the Corral Bar, the local cowboy, rancher, logger, leatherneck tavern. Purpose of being here: to sketch local scenes, local color. The architecture of the Corral is authentic western, so this is why I choose this particular location. I am naive to the consequences of being here.

I have the building penciled in correct perspective and am about to apply ink lines when an old, toothless, denim-overalled cowboy comes and sits beside me.

"Hi. What's ya doin?" he says.

"What does it look like I'm doing?" comes my reply.

"You're cute."

He is a very drunk, old cowboy. An ex-rodeo rider, gold prospector, and logger. A true veteran of the area's resources. I continue in earnest, trying to ignore the old cowboy and concentrate on my perspective. His bony brown hand begins to brush my thigh, then makes a quick grab at my crotch. I jab his hand hard with my pen.

"You'd make a nice mount, good soft legs," he says, smiling, not upset by upsetting me.

I tell him to leave me alone. He won't and I want to finish my drawing, so I tell him to sit in front of me so I can draw him. He does, and I do. As I draw, his hand keeps wandering to my leg, and I have to throw it off with threats that I'm going to leave, then he will be alone again.

He has a quart of beer in his pocket and wants me to go out back with him and drink. His words come with a per-suading little cock of his head and a toothless grin. He is seventy years old. This offer draws a "No" from me, so next he tries offering me five dollars for a "little pussy." I laugh hard and say, "What do you think this is, 1880?" So then he wants me to give it away, says he knows my business.

"Let me pinch your teat," he gums and reaches over to touch me, but I ward away his ancient feeler with a good swift thwack on his arm.

"Awww, come on," he persists, "let me pinch your teat. They can't be any bigger than little green apples."

I get up with my unfinished sketch and leave him sitting on the sidewalk. Down the block some lingering cowboys have been keeping an eye on me. I find out from them that this ancient Romeo is Bill Clayton, age eighty-seven.

✝ **August 11**

Truck-surgery day gets underway. Greg teaches me how to pull the head. I clean it with a scraper bar, air hose, electric drill and brush. Another new experience. Many of Greg's men friends come to watch me work. They stand around while I get covered in grease and gawk like little boys teasing the little girl in the sandbox. I am getting so sick of this breed. The most arrogant of these men asks Greg out for coffee. Greg accepts, asks me to come along, and I do. On the way out, Greg laughs at me and says, "I've never seen a woman roll in the grease the way you have." I wipe grease from my hands with an industrial rag he provided me with, tuck it in my back pocket, and walk across the street to the Cafe with the men.

While drinking coffee, the man who invited us asks me if I'm a "Woman's Libber," to which I reply, "I'm Yvonne, a woman." He tries to get me fired up over defending the issue and says, "It's a bunch of bullshit."

I play docile, not giving him the chance to meet me on the battleground, and say, "Good for you!" My exclamation of affirmation startles him into silence. I win the battle before it even starts. Back at Greg's shop, I glance in the mirror and see my face streaked and smeared almost solid with grease. They drank coffee with me like this, and I didn't know it.

+ August 12

This morning I awoke in tranquility. The quiet sounds of wild ways greeted me, and again, as many times before, I was grateful for this existence. A morning breakfast of granola, peaches, honey, cream. I drank coffee at leisure, then headed up to the building site to stuff insulation between the cracks until Brad awakened and came to work.

Soon Dale came, and we stood on the porch. I asked Dale how to put the paneling up. Brad intervened with his idea. I was not receptive to it or him, and he walked back to his camp. I waited a few minutes, then glanced from the porch to see him take down his tent. I went over and asked, "Brad, what's the matter?" He said, shortly, "It's time for me to leave." And he did leave, only minutes after the encounter that pushed him away. He said he no longer was receiving what he needed from me or from building.

It was no violent departure; in fact, I lent him my truck to drive his things into town, where he was to begin hitchhiking back to Washington, but there was an uneasiness flowing in my stomach. I wanted to cry; I felt he was leaving solely because I was such a horror.

Dale and I had a long lunch, with more talk than food. I did not feel like such a horrible person anymore. The workday was the best so far with Dale. Work and communication, smooth and open. We worked until dark.

Mark came up, announcing his departure for Minnesota in two days. I have decided not to return to Minnesota to live in September, but to winter it here in the cabin. I need to go back, though, to pick up my things, and Mark is my only ticket, even though I am not ready to leave with him yet.

Sitting on the windowless windowsill, I am chewing the decisions of my life. Dale comes to hug me good-bye and massages my neck. It is good to know I have at least one friend.

✝ August 13

Waking this morning, I realize there is no other human's need or schedule to comply with, and this land and I form the only partnership I have. I spend the morning cleaning up Mark's campsite of the trash and other things he has left behind. I work on the porch, totally naked, in the afternoon and putty in a window. I continually glance down the road and expect someone to be walking up, but no one does. Finish nailing up the paneling, struggle with the 4' x 8' sheets of plywood, and realize how big a help Brad was to have around. In the evening I go to town to buy the remaining building supplies I will need for Dale, so he can work on the cabin while I'm back in Minnesota.

We will leave tomorrow, Mark, I, and an unexpected visitor named Laurel, whom Mark has put the eye on and sizes up like she isn't wearing anything. We will drive straight through, drinking coffee to keep on the road . . . Should prove to be an interesting trip.

✛ August 14

We pull from the curb. Mark yells, "Move 'em out!" I am in the open bed of the truck. Laurel and I play along, yelling "Yee-Hawww!" Gravel spins from underneath the tires, and we head out of Pine Valley at 90 mph. Only three miles out of town, we are pulled over by a cop. Mark has been clocked at 78 mph in a 55-mph zone.

Driving through the Malheur National Forest, I feel as if I'm being pulled through a tube of scenery. I take off my shirt, and looking down at my chest, I discover my nipples blend brown with the rest of my skin. Laurel is back with me and is also motivated to remove her shirt. Her breasts, large and white, show the floppy results of their bra confinement. We laugh a lot when the occupants of a passing car stare at the cargo of the little green Datsun pick-up.

Four hours later onto the road, in mid-Idaho, whizzing through endless plains that fade into the dusking horizon, we are clocked and nabbed by the cops for a second time, caught doing 78 in a 55-mph zone. This time, since we are out of state, we have to appear in court. The officer escorts us to a town ten miles away. He is so generous to give us his time.

A silver half-eye of moon hovers over the horizon, striped in setting shades of pink, violet, and blue. An occasional whiff of cow pies confirms our cattle-country location.

We are on the road for 37 hours, in one of which I manage to get some sleep. Behind the wheel, I soar through the Badlands of South Dakota at 90 mph. We make excellent time, stopping only to pee and refuel. We drink beer, coffee, smoke dope, eat cookies and fruit continuously. Just inside the Minnesota border, Mark is caught in the familiar flashing-red spotlight of the law, this time apprehended for doing 80 mph in a 55-mph zone. The officer presents grim-faced Mark with a $44 ticket, which added to the others totals over $120 in speeding tickets.

✛ August 16

This morning the sun completes its ritual of rising, but unlike my view in the mountains of the sun casting its light

113

over tree tops and mountain vistas, here it eases its way through neon and pollution to tower above the IDS building, which I can see from the front window of my sister's apartment, where I have had my first real sleep in two days. When we have had some rest, the three of us go over to Grandpa's and eat buttermilk pancakes with him. He is not the Grandpa I left five months ago. He gurgles in the tubes attached inside his nose. A full-duty nurse is around him all the time. It makes me sad to see this rambunctious old man, who used to take me out fishing at dawn (because I was special, he would always say), now confined to the machines and human hands that sustain him. His eyes no longer sparkle; they are dull with cataracts. He gasps for breath with his 92-year-old lungs.

✛ August 17

Rain bent the broad leaves of the ancient, sinewy elm and dripped down onto the jagged maple branches. Beneath the patchwork quilts of Jay Ellen's bed, I awakened to my first inner city morning in months. Here I do not feel such an absence of the mountains. Jay Ellen and her apartment, fine books and music, fill me.

Last night, dark scents of smoke, alcohol, aftershave, perfume, and bodies—the bar scene: The Town House, a gay bar, predominantly lesbian.

I order a sherry and sip it in a discreet corner, waiting for A. Many stares I feel running up and down my body, wearing cut-offs and a western-cut shirt, unbuttoned enough to reveal a sizeable but concealing wedge of my brown chest. A red kerchief hangs out of my rear pocket. I am a stranger in this gay Barbie-and-Ken fashion world of platform shoes and spangly halter tops—this is what the men wear. The women, the butchy type, have their hair cut very short and wear jeans and vests.

A. comes in the door, which throws light into the dark interior. She quickly discovers me in the corner, approaches without hesitation, and hugs me so hard she lifts me off my feet. I do not like being held this hard. She orders a drink, then sits very close to me—too close; I feel my space is intruded on. I feel awkward and resentful of this casual lover of six months ago. What does she want from me now? It seems more than before, whatever that is. A. tells me she has just broken up with her woman lover of two years.

Our talk carries into the music-filled atmosphere. It is good to talk with A., another woman, a lesbian. Besides electricity and running water, I have missed the compassion and gentle understanding of women. We dance, and a big old bull dyke butts in and wants to dance with me. She cuts right between us and grabs me hard and begins to rub her body all over me. A. intervenes and says to her—she is obviously very drunk—that it was very rude to interrupt us. A small scuffle takes place between them, then we all go to our respective corners of the bar. I begin to feel estranged in this environment and wonder why I ever came. I want to be sitting at my campfire in the mountains, writing.

A group of younger lesbians comes in. I feel more at home with them. A. is twelve years older than I am, of a different dyke culture reflecting some stereotyped ways of loving women that do not coincide with my nature. It is good to see so many women enjoying women, men enjoying men, in this bar scene. My months of seclusion have subdued the gay life. I think about having a gay bar in Pine Valley, then think again, "Not until hell freezes over."

By midnight I am very exhausted, still under the lag from Oregon to Minnesota in the last forty-eight hours. I ask A. to drive me back to Jay Ellen's. A. questions why I want to go there. She has expected me to spend the night with her and wants to drive to Wisconsin and get a motel room. Bluntly I refuse. Even though I've enjoyed her company, I've had enough of it for the night. She reluctantly drives me back, but begins to seduce me in the front seat of her car. I feel the same type of anger with A. over this as I feel with men trying to force themselves on me.

✣ August 19

Yesterday evening I have a flat tire on my bicycle when I am riding past Powderhorn Park. A joint-smoking cyclist passes me, turns around, and stops to offer assistance. He is a fair-skinned, fine-blonde-haired, handsome young man with rimless glasses. He tells me where I can get my tire fixed and walks with me to the cycle shop. We pass a joint on the way. Behind us a voice lets out, "Wow, man, I'm getting a contact high"—from an elderly black lady carrying a bag of groceries.

After my tire gets fixed, Jon, who I've found out has a degree in engineering and is presently studying law, accompanies me to my friend's house whom I was on the way to visit before my tire burst. Dave greets us at the door, a towel draped around his waist, another wrapped around his head. He has just gotten out of the bath. We all sit around enjoying the usual city pastime, drinking, smoking dope, and listening to music. By the time Jon and I leave we are both thoroughly stoned.

Neither of us is ready yet to return to our respective homes—me to Jay Ellen's, Jon to his house. We decide to prolong our chance acquaintance and park our bikes on a grassy knoll above the swings in Powderhorn Park. We talk, and he really listens. I can actually have a conversation with this man. He says that I am an intelligent woman. No man has ever put my intelligence above my sex before. Later, he invites me over to his house across from the park.

Jon is not the beat-around-the-bush, stammer, shammer type. We go upstairs to his bedroom. I am comfortable undressing before him in candlelight. He looks at my body, amazed. "I've never seen a women with so much muscle before," he says.

He makes love strongly, as if he has been starved for affection that is difficult for me to show him in the downbeat of his aggressiveness. This is not the gentle man who has bicycled with me and listened as I talked. I tell him I do not use birth control, which he respects by pulling out before ejaculation.

His touch is hard but not rough. He squeezes me until I am not comfortable. There is little foreplay before he penetrates me. I am not even stimulated, but know by the big gulps of air he takes, Jon has climaxed. Sex is not enjoyable for me, but I don't dislike it, because I like the man. I just don't feel as if I had sex, but that Jon did. I have enjoyed giving him pleasure; he leads a lonely life in his sensitive ways. We sleep in the curled position. I feel secure and warm being held. It is

116

strange for me to share something so sacred to me with a man I have known only for hours.

We wake before dawn and make love once again. He is so happy. I trace the lines of his troll-like smile with my fingertips. I do not enjoy kissing him. It is tactless and reminds me of sucking on warm slugs, but I grit my teeth behind my dissatisfaction of the experience, knowing that it is satisfying him. Maybe I'm unconventional, but I do like the sensitive, stimulating type of kisses that generates fire through my body, not the type of tongue-gagging experience I've just had.

We dress, I get on my bicycle and ride back to Jay Ellen's. Jon gets into his VW van and drives to work. We have set a 7:00 P.M. date this evening to attend a play at the Guthrie.

✢ **August 20**

Yesterday, a full, fine day. I am overwhelmed with people's presence. Bicycle to Metro, tie up school business, visit my secretary friends—they enjoy seeing me and pump me for speech. I walk past my old office, glance inside the oak-framed doorway, see my old typewriter. I laugh as I flash back to my cabin, my axe stuck in a chopping block, my chain saw.

Meet A. for a lunch date. She needs consoling. Thinks I don't love her. I never have, but don't tell her this. I feel pressured with her presence. She drives me in her gold Camaro to the Amazon Bookstore. I have dreamed of this bookstore many days in the mountains, craving women's literature. I pick out three books on lesbianism. Would like to buy three dozen but am on a budget.

At lunch A. has only a cigarette and coffee. I feel uncomfortable with her seek-me-out games. I do not want to be sought out, pulled from the air of reclusivity I keep myself bound in. Since I've returned to Minnesota, many people have sought me out to be with them, friends who enjoy my presence in their lives. This is new for me to feel, this appreciation for me of other people. I wonder what transformation took place inside of me in the mountains.

A. drives me to The Lesbian Resource Center, where I pick up some drawings they have used in a few of their publications of *So's Your Old Lady,* a local lesbian anthology. The women there refer to themselves as "dykes." They wear their hair clipped short. Why do so many women who love women crop their hair and like to be called "dykes"? I am always in contrast in these situations, with my long hair, and the term "dyke" applied to me makes me feel dirty.

On the drive back, A. asks me what label I would put on my sexuality. First I say, "Lesbian," then I feel this isn't true, because I think to be a lesbian means you have to exclude men from your circle of friends, and I don't or even want to. Then I say, "Bisexual," but know this isn't true because to this day I have really only enjoyed having sex with women and always feel more closely drawn to women in compassion than to men.

By this time I am really flustered. I don't know what to call myself. Does this mean I don't know who I am? So I tell A. I want the label my parents gave me, Yvonne Mary Pepin. How come it is, I wonder, that one needs a label in the city to display one's identity? No wonder so many people have identity crises, what with all the different names they can choose to tape onto themselves.

In the evening a knock at Jay Ellen's back door brings in Jon, smiling, his features soft. He says, "Wow!" and keeps a glowing expression on his face directed at me. I forget that I am wearing a dress, which is why his face turns the way it does. Yes, a dress. This lumberjack, log-cabin builder, macho woman removes her piney denims and plaids and wears a dress that falls in soft folds to the floor, the "V" neckline pointing open short of my breasts. I feel good wearing it and realize this side of me is one facet I neglected out of practicality in the past months as a builder. With all my macho feats and boasting, I enjoy this soft side of me that likes wearing jewelry and fine clothes. I feel, for lack of a better word, feminine.

Jon opens the door, looking sharp and sleek in his attire. I do not protest his gesture, as is my normal way around door-opening men. We arrive at the Guthrie three minutes before curtain call, looking like the perfect young couple but very stoned from the joint we smoked on the drive, and are ushered to our red velvet seats by a blue-coated usher. It is

118

premiere night of *Mother Courage,* a wonderfully acted play. At intermission we have a drink in the lobby with the rest of the Barbie and Ken dolls.

✝ **August 21**

People make the city and my time here happy, like the tamaracks dancing in the mountain wind. There are so many characteristics, ideas, life styles here, just as there are species of flora and fauna in the forest.

Many people now seek me out. I learn from them what to take and give back. We are hosts to catalysts in others; dandelions gone to seed, we blow into the hearts of others, take root, wither, blossom, or die. I do not feel negative about myself the way I did when Jean and Tony were living on my land. I guess I am not as bad as I thought. Something must have changed in me, inner and outer, during my months of mountain seclusion. Three men in the last two days have asked me to spend the weekend in the country with them. Two of the men, old friends who said, "Take care, kid," when I left for the mountains, now, like Jon, refer to me as a "Fine lady."

A. takes me out to hear music at the Riverside Cafe this evening. I am so high during the show, not just from dope but with myself and the integration with people, I boogie in a stationary position with the music. Once in a while I laugh in my own elation. I have too many emotions to describe and explode frequently inside with happiness.

A. again, after the show, wants me to spend the night with her, then persists. I'm only nineteen and being hustled by women and men. Wonder what I'll be like when I'm twenty.

✝ **August 22**

Ultimately, everyone is looking for the ultimate mate, aren't they? Why must we? I notice everyone in the city seems to be attached to another person or if not, looking for an attachment. Why can't one sustain oneself by one's self instead of relying on another to fill the void, meet the need?

Jean, I learn, has returned to Minnesota, has left Tony. I

want to call her. Is this a sign of my weakness or my strength? I want to tell her I forgive her for all the games she played with me, that I have been very hurt, but have grown strong through my pain. I want her to see this strength inside of me. Because a person has been butchered by a lover, does this warrant not showing that lover scraps of love that remain?

+ **August 24**

Had another very active day yesterday, partying with friends. Blew myself up last night. The pieces are still sifting back down into what's left of my mind and body. It seems all my social contacts in the city hinge on the consumption of alcohol and dope.

Roxy picks me up on her Kawasaki 400, and we roar out to Chanahassen, the land of condominiums. Roxy drives 95 mph as much as she can, and my nose is pushed flat against my face with the speed. At her apartment, one of those with a sauna and pool, we proceed to waste ourselves. I bake a pan of marijuana brownies with a whole lid of dope in them. I eat half the pan in one hour and am on a different planet by the time the rest of our party arrives to go to the bar. we drink a bottle of wine on the short walk there.

Inside, a band is sweating on a tiny stage, moving their electrified instruments in rhythm with their convulsing bodies. The music is so loud it vibrates through my bones. Everyone talks by shouting. I get irritated in this mode of strained communication and quit talking, just sit observing the insanity that gets more insane as people crowd in, become drunk, drunker, while the effect of the brownies I ate consumes my rational mind. The peak of my inability to cope with it all comes when some friends ask me to play this board game where you drop in a quarter, a little light flashes on the screen, and you try to play hockey with the light. Watching the light bounce back and forth and people's total enthusiasm over the game sends me ablitz. I cannot relate. I flash back to my campfires and whittling a stick with my pocketknife.

I get the heck out of that bar as fast as I can scram through the crowds. Two friends join me, and we head for Roxy's

apartment, to the hot sauna. I think perspiring will help clear me like a mountain sweat does. I need to find some answers, some insight to all the activity that has blown up my quiet centered self. I need to become more in touch with my heart beat, senses, and organs that the city has diffused. There are two things essential: to be close to the land, and quiet in and around myself. I extend myself in the sauna until I almost pass out. I don't know whether it is from drugs or heat or a combination of the two.

Feeling a need to find some answers to calm the swirling in my mind, I go outside and find comfort on the apartment lawn. I sit there naked, trying not to be pulled out of myself by the lights and passing cars. Suddenly a "Hey you" curdles what silence I have been trying to tranquilize myself with. I realize I am naked in public, forgetting, because of my mountain indoctrination, to wear clothes after a sweat. I make a mental note not to show my privates in public and to brush up on my list of social taboos.

✛ August 26

Again I realize—I relearn—the difficulties in being the woman I want to grow into. Making people understand I am not crazy for wanting solitude in the mountains is not an act of conversation but a battle of convincing everyone who doubts my capabilities that I am capable of withstanding what I create for myself. I will be who I want to be, because I am sure of my identity.

✛ August 27

Yesterday morning Jon comes early to pick me up to canoe down the St. Croix. On the drive in the van, Jon pulls out two tiny pink dots from some tinfoil, LSD, and we each down one. Jon has decided to skip law school tonight and spend a whole day canoeing. He steers the van towards an inlet of the river, and I experience the familiar signs, chilled nose tip, my teeth gritting down. The open patchwork fields and meadows, the curly-topped trees, all become surrealistic; the various shades of green complement one another.

The river is deserted when we launch the canoe. We are Tom Sawyer and Huck Finn of the counterculture, floating down the river, passing a fine bottle of rosé, neither of us wearing shirts. Trees dance in the wind and beckon me from the canoe to join them on the shore, where they bend and reach out to me. They whisper that I am the tree savior and must help all trees. The land is what I need, what I must help take care of. People have gotten too far away from their origins; they have scarred the skin of their mother in consumptive greed—open pit mining, the Alaskan pipeline, asphalt and concrete. Through neglect she withers and dies before eyes that seek technological advancements, the greenback god. If I am gentle and considerate with the earth, she will treat me accordingly. Through her I will learn my strengths and virtues.

Jon sits in the stern, his body's colors, pastel, blend finely with the other colors of the day. I look at his facial features; they are young and old in a turn of his head, revealing a handsome man. He is my preconceived vision of a male lover. I think how I want to keep this relationship pure, not have it become a washout like the others I've had with men.

We beach the aluminum canoe on a deserted sandbar, collapse in the warm sand together and make love intensely. I am more relaxed and passive due to the effects of the acid, and everything is a sensual experience—the warm sand that hugs me, the wind that gushes between us. I do not fully realize we have had intercourse until I feel warm sperm fall out of me and onto the sand, making miniature balls. We wash in the river and eat a picnic lunch.

The birth control question enters my mind. Whose responsibility is it? Mine or his? He has not even asked about or made the proper precautions. There is no safe or easy method of birth control for women; that is why I don't like to bother with it. But if I relate anymore with Jon, I will have to. With all the atoms split and men sent to the moon, you would think they could invent a sound method of birth control for women and men. But the responsibility rests with women, while the men reap profits off the pills they push, the babies they scrape. Men aren't concerned with safe birth control for women; all they want is to get their rocks off.

Jon keeps asking me all day to stay with him in Minnesota

instead of returning to the mountains. I keep telling him no, that this does not mean I don't love him, but I need to find out about myself in relation to myself before I'm able to have a relationship with anyone else. We paddle home. I take the stern and correct Jon's use of the word "sternsman" with "sternsperson." Sometimes I paddle too fast for Jon, and he tells me, instead of struggling to keep up.

Back at Jon's house, we lie naked in bed watching television—not actually watching it, but it was turned on. I tell Jon I am not using birth control and won't, so he must be responsible for himself and me. He restrains during intercourse and ejaculates into a kleenex afterwards, throwing the soggy wad into the wastebasket. It makes a thud sound.

I ask him to help me drive to Pine Valley, because I don't feel safe pulling a loaded trailer by myself. He says he wants to but doesn't know if he can get the time off work. We fall asleep on the strip of his mattress and sleep in the curled inside-outside position. Waking in the morning, he says first thing, "I'll check at work today,"—meaning he is certainly considering the drive.

I've many things to tie together before I set my plans in action to journey home to Oregon.

+ **August 28**

Got my car out of storage and on the road after some minor adjustments. I'm so used to driving the ¾-ton tank that the Gremlin felt like a toy. I had a 6:30 dinner date with Jon this evening, and entered the rush of traffic that swept me across town to his house, where we tuned up the car. We drank a bottle of Liebfraumilch on the couch afterwards.

He is always saying, "Why don't you stay in Minnesota? Will you stay in Minnesota? I want you to stay in Minnesota." I am getting tired of dealing with this; it causes a strain on my affections for him. Lately I've become irritated by his constantly touching me, which seems to be a direct outpouring of his desire for me. I will have to learn to control my anger and impatience; I do not want this relationship ruined by my bitchiness.

✝ August 30

The sun rose orange and pink over the hills and plateaus of the Black Hills. How did they get the name "Black Hills"? Jon and I filled the thermos at Wall Drug. We have been on the road since leaving the city at 8:00 P.M. last evening. The drive so far has been relaxing. I had a lot of anxiety in the beginning of the trip because of the extra two thousand pounds we're towing. The load is definitely too heavy for the car; the engine runs hot all the time.

In Lusk, Wyoming, we bought a half gallon of chocolate ice cream and a pint of brandy. We poured it all into a pitcher and drank the cocktail while driving through the hot Wyoming plains. I wasn't wearing a shirt, and all the passing truckers honked their horns at me.

✝ September 1, 1975

With the morning air crisp, a fire does much to advance the pleasure of my day. I am home, and everything I left lies where I left it. When we rounded the last bend of the road last night, the cabin stood there glowing, welcoming me home. My old friends the tamaracks and ponderosa seemed changed with fall's approach.

We made love in the tent last night, both relieved that the long drive was behind us. I am not responsive to Jon's affection. I think I will not be able to have a good sexual relationship until I've done many things in the future to help me grow into the woman I want to be. A fulfilling relationship with another takes time and much giving. I would rather be taking the time and giving to myself. With Jon, the issue of birth control blocks my spontaneity in loving him. I'm angered all the time that there are not safe alternatives for women and that women, it seems, must make all the necessary precautions and jeopardize their health in the process. Loving another woman is so much more spontaneous than loving a man. There never is any premeditated birth control to deal with. Even though Jon is gentler than any man I've ever been with before, I still do not feel the comfort with him that I have felt in loving women. Sex with Jon is a task. He is in and out in minutes, rarely using foreplay. I think he is still under the educated influence of the "Vaginal Orgasm." He has had eight years of college, has received his degree in engineering, is going into law, but is ignorant of a woman's clitoris.

At about 8:00 A.M. we both get up and eat breakfast beside the campfire. After breakfast I tell Jon of my desire to write; he understands and goes for a walk. I think it is very intuitive that he should understand my need to be alone. I wonder if he will always respect it.

✝ September 2

"Flight 379" blares over the airport too quickly; it breaks the dream and sends Jon turning to exit through gate number 3. When he finally moves to board his plane in the Idaho airport, I hug him harder than ever before, my tears absorbing into the front of his pastel-plaid shirt. "Get out of here," I say, hug him harder, then snap my sweater at him. He leaves. I am amazed at myself, at this tearful display of emotion.

✝ September 3

I was cold and depressed last night unloading the truck in the dark. I realized how I had come to rely on Jon's support, how I missed his presence. It seems I once again must acclimate myself to solitude. I told myself that being depressed about unloading the truck in the dark was not doing me any good, so I better get moving, it would warm me up, and I unloaded the last five-gallon can full of kerosene.

Did my first real day's work on the cabin in three weeks. It felt good to get back into the rhythm of swinging tools. With luck I should start chinking tomorrow. I came close to being creamed by a falling ladder this afternoon. The near accident sharply increased my awareness of being alone and the consequences of an injury.

✝ September 5

"If we are to arrive at any blytheness in facing life, we must have faith to believe that it is exercising this gift, in living it out to its fullest that she achieves herself, that she justifies her existence." —Ruth Benedict, 1887-1948

Amber currents flow over plains of mustard yellow. I dribble honey over my thick pan cornbread. Flies and bees touch down on my lunch, and I whisk them away with an angry hand. "Get away from me, you creeps." After only seconds, I realize that they are not creeps but creatures like me, seeking sustenance. I pour some honey on a rock, hoping they will retreat from my bread before I eat one of them.

First job of the day: mix mortar, the cement paste I slap, or rather carefully trowel, between the wall cracks. I have never mixed mortar before. I have never chinked up log walls before with the mortar I am learning to mix to the proper consistency by trial and error.

Into the wheelbarrow: 2 shovelsful of cement, 7 shovelsful of washed sand, 1 or half a shovelful of lime; pour in water until the hoe mixes the contents to a consistency that only trial and error will declare proper to adhere between the cracks. After I have a wheelbarrow of this mixed, I shovel it into my bucket, tuck the trowel in my back pocket, and haul the heavy thing up two rickety ladders into the loft. I fill my hock with mortar, a hock which I had to make for myself, as the ones in the store had handles too huge to close my hand around. Another case where men's tools—and that's who it seems tools were designed for—like work gloves, do not fit my needs. They are too cumbersome, built to accommodate the larger physique of men. In order for me to work in a "man's" world, I must find the tools that work for me.

From the hock, I scrape mortar with my trowel between

the cracks, pat it in, and smooth the gray plaster to a finish. If the mortar is too dry, it will fall out; if too wet, seep out. I experiment in frustration with the mortar's make up until I discover that somewhere in between dry and soupy lies the mortar of my desire. If I come across a nail that needs pounding in so the trowel will glide smoothly over the surface, I hammer it in, only to have the mortar I've just applied all fall out.

A note to future chinkers of log cabins: Make sure all the nails are pounded in before you begin to chink. Chinking is not as romantic as I had imagined it to be. It is hard, dirty, monotonous work.

✤ September 6

The day's motions are most conspicuously ingrained on my hands. These pinkies that came back from the city a week ago have been transformed into dry, cracked gray claws. Mortar exacts a great toll on the condition of my flesh.

The wheelbarrow, hock, shovel, hoe, trowel all scraped clean for the day, my pants dusted of the dried mortar. I bathe in the creek and shiver in the fall air. I apply hand lotion to all parts of my body, dried out from the mortar. Lying in my tent tonight, I am totally exhausted, feeling the day's hauling in my bones, which just ease onto the sleeping bag. I lie on my back, basking in candle glow—the colors, this atmosphere so pleasing, I do not feel as if I'm alone.

✤ September 7

Alas,
this chinking
is a pain
in the ass.

I am careless today and do not block the ladder when I scale up to the gable peak to repound some nails. My neglect pays off when the ladder slides to the side with me on it. My fortune is such that I am able to grab between the log cracks instead of falling, but I am left hanging on the wall, twenty feet from the ground. I press myself flat against the wall like a mountain climber descending a sheer rock cliff. I lower myself enough to maintain a footing on the windowsill and then jump to the ground.

I take a lunch break and think about accidents and how they kill people. The day to this point has been terrible. I want to write a book called "How Not to Build a Log Cabin."

It's All Herstory

I buy a splitting wedge
half-inch
nylon rope . . .

"What, may
I ask,
are you
planning to do
with these?"

Paunch-bellied man
with a big
pored nose,

he says,

"That's not for
women,"

after I say,
"splitting,
chopping,
hauling
logs . . ."

he says,

"out here
women bake
bread, babies,

men
chop wood,
work"

I smile

"That's the way
it's supposed
to be!"

he says.

I smile.

My bones feel
the content
and strain

from lifting
logs, splitting wood,
lifting 50-pound
boxes of galvanized nails,
94-pound bags
of Portland cement.

"Men's work."

I smile
at his
ignorance.

+ September 8

Just finished work—had to—the spaces between the logs were as dark as the night. Night comes early now; around 7:30 P.M. there is not enough light to see without aid of artificial or fire illumination.

Dale came today and finished notching down the porch rafters. I chinked half a wall. I have to put chicken wire between some of the cracks; they are so large, the mortar will not hold in. Troweling mortar over chicken wire is easier than over nails. A note to all chinkers: chicken wire before nails.

Tamarack, who ran away from Dale's place when I was in Minnesota, is home tonight. Tamarack showed up in a culvert this morning between the Doc's and the Johnson's. Dale heard meowing and stopped his truck to find Tamarack waiting to be driven up the remaining few miles to me. That feline friend had walked over 35 miles to come home.

+ September 9

"What kind of work is this for a woman of intelligence?" I ask myself tonight, sitting in front of the campfire, looking like an old prospector who has just come in grimy and exhausted from the digs. I mix mortar, haul mortar, trowel mortar, clean up after the mortar, do it again and again and again, mortar, mortar, more mortar. I'm turning into a mortar moron with the monotony of this work.

+ September 10

How I live and live, but never fully realize that I am living until I slow down enough to take into my senses what I've lived. In my hurry to do this so I can hurry to do that, I lose perspective on what I really am up here living for: a simple, direct contact with my self and nature.

I quit work before dark tonight and sat on the porch just to listen and feel, not to think about what has to get done or isn't getting done by my taking time out. My senses expanded at the vista from this porch. The ash berries, which only last week speckled the bushes red, have fallen and left only a few dots of their reminders behind on the branches. The tamar-

acks have already begun their yellow turn into autumn and are letting fall their yellow needles. Signs of winter show in the forest's changing colors. I feel the solidity of the cabin underneath my bottom seep into my bones. I feel the care and determination in this wood.

I analogize the constant sound of the creek with "muffled multitudes of cellophane wrinkling." My solitude hits with direct impact. I am feeling the forest, hearing and seeing her in ways that were drowned out by the constant motion of cabin construction. The night animals speak in a different voice than they did in the months of May, June, and July. Coyotes crying in the distance make cold currents of electricity run through my spine. There are the sounds of bat flutter and goshawk scream. But the sounds I cannot decipher or attach to a recognizable form, those that are left to my imagination, make me tense in what I cannot see.

✝ September 11

An early morning, one that makes me aware of the worth of being. On the way to town, I stop and pick apples in the Doc's meadow. In Pine Valley, I run errands quickly, efficiently. Is it my imagination, or are people smiling at me as I saunter the pavement and weave in and out of stores, quick as air.

Jake Gray tells me he does not like my idea of wintering it alone. "Too many things can go wrong too fast, and it will be too late before anyone can get to you." I banter with him for a while, trying to assure him of my capabilities. I wonder, though, if I were a man, would he still have his doubts about my winter caper? Regardless of his doubts, he says that I've much intelligence, and he admires me more than any person he knows.

Thelma Hampstead, Sam's wife, also says, "Honey, give up now and go back to Minnesota where it's warm," when I tell her of my intentions to winter it alone. I am determined to prove to them I can do what I set out to do.

✝ September 13

Again, discouragement. I spend my days working from sunup to sundown, never getting on top of this endless pile of work.

I am on the porch putting in a window this afternoon when I hear a horn. I quickly put a shirt on, thinking I have visitors, but when I see it is only Mark in his green Datsun, I take my shirt off again. I think, "What the hell are you doing beeping your horn in my solitude?" I know there is something wrong, though, when he pulls himself out of the truck and yells, "Get your shirt on!"

At his truck, I see a red rope tied around his leg. Then I notice the red extends up and down his pantleg. Without saying, "What happened?" I just tell him to get in.

Blood is dripping onto the ground, running from his leg. A pool has accumulated on the truck floor during his short drive up from Ann's cabin, where he sliced a main artery in his leg while chopping wood.

Never in my many journeys down this rutty mountain road have I pushed the accelerator as hard as I do now. Mark is propped up in the back, his leg elevated by some pillows I stuffed under it. I spew gravel on the county road, driving 70 mph, realizing that my brother could be/is bleeding to death. Twenty stitches later and five veins tied off, Mark is alive. We are in the emergency room of the Blue Mountain Hospital. Vain I normally am of my appearance, but nonetheless I'm proud now, wearing my dusty dungarees, plaid shirt, mortar-speckled boots, some of the leather splashed with my brother's blood. I am not the "immaculate conception" that the nurses are.

Mark's accident only intensifies the reality that an occurrence of a similar nature could befall me. Would I be able to drive for help if I did not faint at the sight of my own blood?

✝ September 16

The last few days, I've been dubious about my winter solitude. Will I, can I endure this aloneness?

✝ September 19

Tamarack makes a fine specimen of a feline, sitting silhouetted on a rock, warming himself by the night campfire. Something is not right when I hear a sizzle that does not sound like wood aflame. Tamarack's tail has caught on fire. He runs flaming into the night. I run directly behind him to capture my burning feline friend and extinguish the flames.

If he were not in pain right now and I did not have to cuddle up against the revolting smell of burned fur, I would find the situation of a flaming cat running in a moonlit night, being chased by a young woman, very amusing.

✝ September 20

I moved into the cabin today. I smell of many days' work. The cabin is empty with the exception of the stove, which has a fire in it now, my cherrywood desk, a small maple night-stand that holds my kerosene lamp, and my bedding strewn before the fire.

Starkness is the overpowering element in here tonight. The yellow glow from the lamp and orange crackle of flame in the fireplace warm only one section of this cabin in illumination and leave the rest in cast shadows. Outside, I see light spill from the windows onto the ground in bent yellow sections. I am not very content tonight. Tamarack kept me awake all last night, and I am very tired. Although I should be, I'm not overjoyed with my first night inside the cabin.

✝ **September 21**

No inspiration, but oh, do I need some. Diagnosis of my situation: mental stagnation. Too many tedious, mindless days filled with chinking. Too many days of body-consuming, mind-thwarting work that leaves the body strained, the brain drained of inspiration.

Like a muscle not used, my mind atrophies, accumulates a roll of fat through inactivity, leaving it stale as bad breath, an after-effect of something partaken, of an unsavory constitution; leaving it stale and lethargic, hanging, like a dumpling woman's pendulous breasts.

What causes my mood fluctuations? My discontent? Does

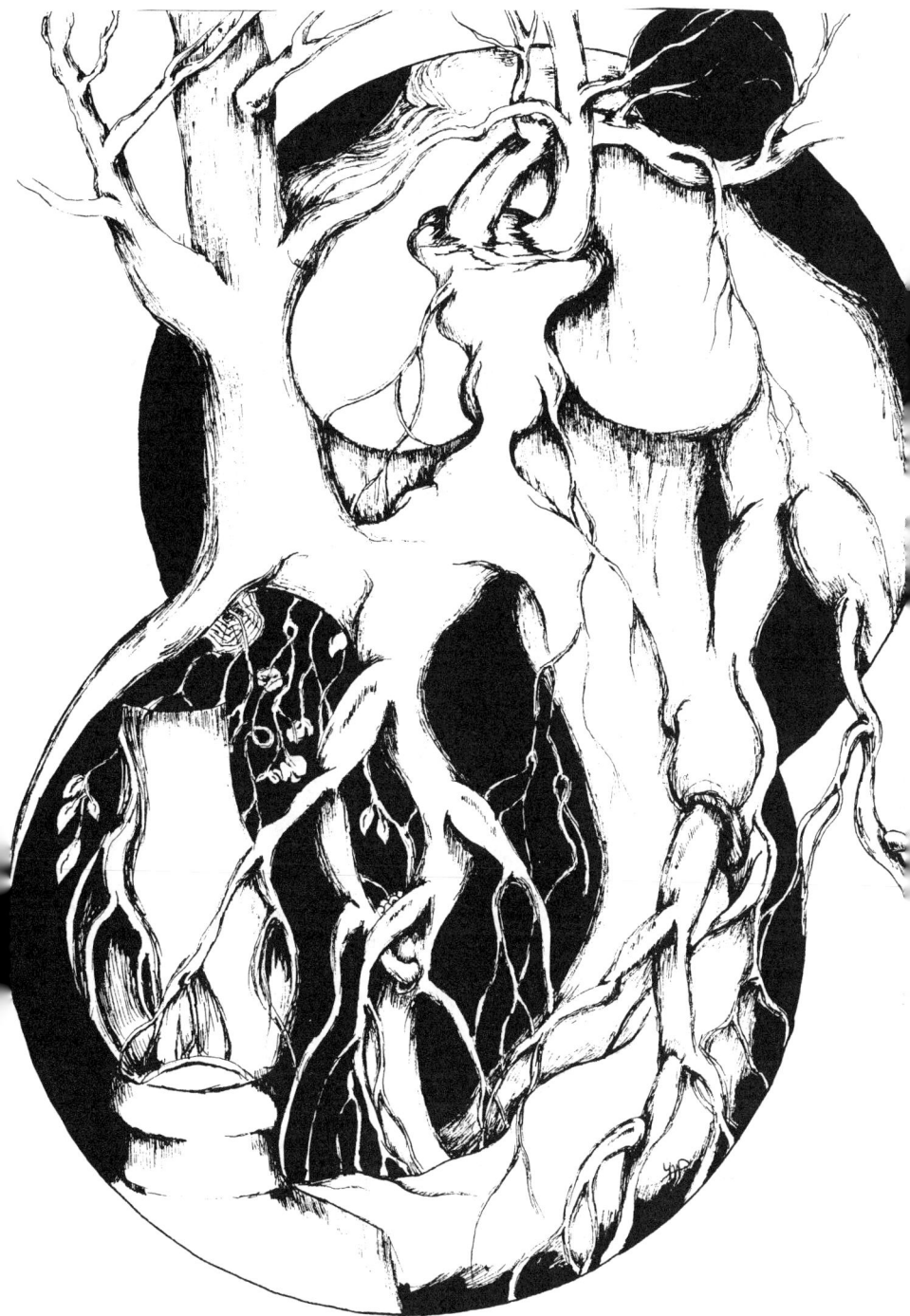

life always have to present itself tap dancing in order for me to reflect a worthwhile image of myself?

I wonder if it is not the cycle of moon slicing the ink sky, the eerie wind whipping the tamaracks, the flare of fire, my aloneness, this all-encompassing aloneness, that curtail the breathing of my complacence?

✝ September 23

I cannot sleep in the night. The moon, looking like an 88-cent ball with a kicked-in side, slithers her light through my loft window and winds my mind in her mystical motion, where I am pulled from the nocturnal slumber required to create a healthy human specimen. I am dragged by the force of moonlight into those shadows only the moon can throw. The moon—awake on a black satin blanket over a million polished pinheads.

I lick cheese from my fingertips. I have just eaten a thick piece of cheddar along with some hoops of sliced onion. They told me in town this combination acts as a sedative. Insomnia is the force that beckons me from my bed. So much onion and cheese I consume; still I am saucer-eyed. Sleep will not come, has not come since the first night I moved into this cabin.

✝ September 24

I slept last night, eight hours, but am exhausted from the previous two sleepless nights. Perhaps insanity's insomniac pull has released me for a while.

✝ September 29

There is this aloneness in the night that no one—because there is no one—can buffer me from. I am alone in the hollow face of day, in her dark subconscious version of life. If there are feelings in me during these hours—like a bellyache or heartache or quivering mind—that need compassion, companionship, I do not let myself feel the feeling. To feel would be to acknowledge need. To acknowledge the need would

136

send me up front, on the line, to face the truth that I have created my reality so that there be no one to fill my needs.

This aloneness in my night shines like the moon's image caught in the curve of the kerosene lamp globe. It is bent, distorted, a reflection out of the ordinary. An image transcended by the eye awake with the night, looking inside where there is no light, finding light inside where there has been no light.

Tonight I look at myself framed by the two flames of the lamps. My immediate features, articulate in the direct light, reflect in the windowpane. I stare outside at the moon and am diffused into the dark background; only my immediate features—eyes, mouth, nose, long fine hair—stand out. The rest of me has been dispelled in the dark life beyond me.

Through this reflection, I look to myself for the comfort I may need, the comfort only I have the power to provide. But I feel no need for comfort, content in my darkened image. My eyes are the light on my face, innocent, intense. I do not seem to be now who I have been. I am recognizable to myself only through the distinguished features attributed to the parents whose fusion created me. My mother's eyes are here tonight, and my father's forehead.

When one is reaching, one must find what is to be found or become dissatisfied with what has not been found. I continue to stretch when it seems there is nothing left to be found— and I find myself.

✝ September 30

I am making myself work it out, this mood that overtakes my surface self and turns me inside, brooding. I work hard in the day so that I may sleep in the night. The outside of the cabin is nearly chinked; inside I have fitted molding strips I ripped with the chain saw. I have shoveled an outhouse pit, 4' x 4' x 4'. I have begun to collect firewood.

So I made it through the day—no feat since it is being done by millions of others, consistently, in every curve of the earth. But I am a queer little coot and survive by my wit and will in seclusion and communicate with the nib of pen and blank paper to fill with my biased, self-oriented conversations.

✝ October 1, 1975

I quit my indulgence in diversity, quit work that was de-feating spontaneity of spirit with the land, and took a noon-day run. I wore only buckskin-colored Adidas and traversed the meadows and mountainsides in the meandering intensity of fall's sun rays. In a pool that was almost up to my neck, I bathed the sweat from my skin. At least a dozen trout dispersed. A delicacy of my life is my freedom to run.

Level the outhouse, linseed oil the countertops, sharpen the chain saw, hang some pictures, clean house, clear brush from a path to drag logs over for firewood, build shelves, organize my belongings inside the cabin, saw and split wood, begin to shake the roof—and then there are daily chores to contend with.

✝ October 2

Its screams are opaque, glassy, horrible—cries in the black. There is no escape for the creature and its batting, beating of wings inside the mantle, where flame consumes and cremates. The sounds of a burning moth linger long after its cremation. I watch it until it becomes ash. I hear a solitary plane fly over-head. The stovepipe creaks. These are the sounds accompany-ing me tonight.

Today has been a bushel basket of activity. At 5am

Hampstead's Mill, I jump into a huge pile of planer shavings. We talk about Sam's boyhood in Canada, how he was ripped off last week, his hard times, insulation, apples, hand generators, and 45 minutes later I mention the reason for coming. "Yes," he has my boards ready and is happy that I have listened to him. I have learned, in this way of rural America, to listen even if the topic of conversation is not of interest, because between the words lie answers to questions. Though this method is very time-consuming, it allows one to come into valuable bits of information. If I had worn my "Let's do business" attitude in front of Sam, I never would have gotten the lead from him on where I can borrow a hand generator or an aluminum extension ladder.

Drive to Pine Valley, buy window latches, weatherstripping. Meet Pete at the post office; he asks me to join him for lunch. I have tea while he eats huge portions of meat. Take my driver's test and pass with an 87; now I am truly an Oregonian. I have a new muffler welded on the tank and eat a pint of ice cream while waiting.

I park my truck below my land and walk up, the day is so beautiful. I take off my clothes and walk free, pure and simple as the winds rasping pine needles. Twice I halt my footsteps to honor the four directions, my arms outstretched in recognition of the spirit in all that surrounds me, that moves me. Even though I am totally alone—no one is around for miles, I feel full, not longing, content with the presence of trees, breeze and grasses. The openness of the day holds me. "Alone" is defined by being the only person in presence.

Back home, I bathe in the creek, then begin the horrendous job of maneuvering the 40-foot extension ladder. I climb to my destination, shouldering a full pallet of mortar, I scale the ladder unsurely. I have never worked this high before. The increase in height and occasional wobble from the ladder scare me. I sweat from fear and exertion. This ladder has the extra added length I need to reach the gable ends, but up this high I am worried about falling and killing myself. I take precautions and clear the ground of anything that I may fall down on top of. I premeditate my actions in case of a fall. I will push myself away from the ladder in order not to

complicate my injuries by being tangled up in the rungs of the aluminum ladder. In an unplanned descent, I will let my body go limp in the air to lessen the degree of impact of flesh on ground. It is doubtful that all this premeditation would come in handy if this ladder were to slip and fall. The action would occur so fast I wouldn't have time to put my plans to work. I would just be a pile of bones through pierced flesh on the earth before my senses would perceive the fall.

✝ **October 3**

Celebration of a New-Way-to-Pee Day!

Being that the night brings darkness and a drastic decline in temperature, it is a bothersome and loathsome task to leave the warmth of this cabin in the mid of night to venture up to the outhouse to irrigate my bladder. I discover tonight, out of not wanting to get wet in the cold rain falling outside, how to pee in a coffee can.

✝ **October 4**

It is a gray morning. Ferocious winds blow the yellow

needles and dead leaves skyward, leaving the trees spun like naked skeletons. The sullen scene makes me feel lonely. I get out of bed, but back in again, with a book. The morning is good for nothing but reading. Like a fine bottle of wine kept on the back rack and stored until opened for the special occasion, I break the binding on *Patience and Sarah* by Isabel Miller. I snuggle under the quilts, absorbed in the book.

✦ October 5

The morning is again marbled gray. Outside is an ocean of pine-needle surf crashing under a wind-turbulent sky. I have finished reading *Patience and Sarah*. It leaves me feeling warm like the stovetop. It also makes me lonesome for sharing. I long for a gentle woman to help me chink, chop wood, sharpen the chain saw, haul water—the day-to-day chores of mountain life. I want to share conversation around the fire and know quiet moments with another, have another love me but allow me the freedom to be me.

Took a long walk this afternoon. The sun came out to shine on spurts of yellow and red leaves thrown up by fall wind gusts. In the distant mountains I heard gunshots. This abruptly made me realize today is the third day of hunting season.

Everywhere in the valley I am confronted with my opposition to hunting. The majority of the natives hunt. They hate protectors of animals like me. I am ridiculed because I choose not to eat meat. The people who eat meat think it is unhealthy for me not to eat meat. I tell them it is not for health reasons I chose to quit, but moral. I do not like killing.

The men who ridicule me run the mountains like little boys with their rifles, trick or treating the wilds for goodies to fill their game bags. They dress in seasonal costumes of orange and red so they will not shoot each other. They leave the grounds littered with empty beer bottles.

✦ October 6

Dorothy cuddles Jimmie's fevered brow to her breast. Will sits adjacent to them, reading the Sunday newspaper. The

Johnsons are the first people I ask to come to the cabin-warming party next Sunday. Yes, they will be there anytime after 1:00.

I proceed on my invitational adventure and invite the Grays, Greg Anderson and family, Frank Miller and family, the Hampsteads, Parkers, and the Doc and Jill. I will ask others who have helped me and shown me friendship along the way. At first I am skittish around others today, not knowing if I should speak first or if I should maintain eye contact. It is queer to feel uncomfortable with people.

✝ October 7

Pain and discouragement exist in me as frequently as the cold gray rains come. Finding that despair captures too many of my secluded moments makes me churn over the decision of whether it is right for me to live this way.

Dale came to work today and brought Sophie. They left early, though; the rains were too heavy to work in. I tried to chink, but rain filled my wheelbarrow with water, diluting the mortar before I had a chance to apply it between the cracks. The wools I wore were also saturated, but I stayed fairly warm. Soon the downpour pushed me inside the cabin, where I kindled myself warm in front of the fire and drank hot tea.

This is really the first day I have appreciated the protection of the cabin. This is the first day I have needed to find shelter in my dwelling. Waiting for the rains to subside, I sharpened the chain saw, steel-wooled the tools. Towards evening it was just a drizzle, so I went back to chinking.

Perched on the top ladder rung, I was a plaid-shirted Statue of Liberty, clutching the eternal pallet of mortar. I was chinking the last few spaces on the gable end, then the cabin would be chinked tight inside and outside. I glanced down at the red rubber tip of the aluminum ladder just in time to see it slowly slip down from the wall it was resting against.

Everything happened so fast that there was not time to enact my "What to do if the ladder falls" plan. My stomach and heart pushed up into my throat as I fell. It seemed an eternity before I hit the ground, but it was actually seconds before I felt the contortion and pain from the hard impact. I didn't know whether I was dead or alive, broken or not. I think I must have been knocked out for a while, because I came to, surfacing through layers of body pain until I could localize. I thought I had broken my collarbone, arm, leg, shin. The pain intensified as I lay there in the rain, splattered with mortar, my upturned face being washed of the hot tears that were running down my cheeks. I gave little moans and convulsed in tears that I tried to suppress, then finding no reason to suppress them, just let myself cry.

I could not move. I thought I would have to lie there and die in the winter snows that would cover me before anyone would come to find me—just bones etched into the spring ground. I did not want to lie there and die, after all I'd gone through to get the cabin to where it was. So close to the end, I had only a few more spaces to chink on the highest gable end, the one I had just fallen almost forty feet down from.

I was a helpless sight, pitiful and crunched on the muddy earth. I was dirty and wet, crying. But I knew I was going to be all right when I glanced over at the ladder, also getting rained on, and yelled, "Fuck you!"

I tried to distinguish where my injuries were and concluded the sharpest pains lay in my chest, elbow, and knee. In slow motion I reran the fall in my memory. It was like descending in a strobe light. I remembered smacking down on top of the hock. I looked over to my side then and saw the handle severed from the four 16-penny nails that had held the pallet in place. I had broken off the handle with my chest. In the five minutes I lay on the ground, rolling in wet sawdust, mortar, and mud, the only warmth I experienced was from the hot tears flowing down my face before the rainfall quickly washed them into the earth.

I summoned all that had not been knocked out of me by the fall, hoisted myself painfully to my feet and dragged into the cabin. I was still crying in hot, angry bursts. Inside, I examined my wounds. There was a very dark bruise, growing redder and purpler, about two inches above my left breast; this was where I fell on the pallet. Two inches lower would have turned me into an Amazon. Both my shins were bloody;

transparent onion peels of skin rolled back and revealed Swiss dot patterns of blood. My elbow, from what I could see of it, was bloody; it would not swivel far enough for me to see anything but wet and caked blood. My back and neck were just beginning to awaken in throbbing sensations.

By now the tears have stopped and I wash my wounds. I am somber and discouraged. I do not know if I should return to work or rest myself after the fall. There is, I know, a possibility of internal injuries. I must become my own doctor and listen. My aches say, "Stay inside, stay quiet, keep warm." My best friend says, "You've just had a bad fall, take it easy." The mother in me says, "Nurture yourself." But my will, the part of me that drives me, says, "Get back up there, get to work, you're not hurt bad. After all, a man would do it." But some voice of my rational self says, "You're not a man, you're a woman with a woman's sensibilities, a woman's body."

This bothers me, that I do not know which voice inside me to listen to. I do not want to pamper myself. How many people take a fall like this, then get right back up and work? How many people even live through a fall like this? How do I gauge my limitations, my assertions? How do I know when and where to stop before catastrophe occurs? Is this an example of what it is to use common sense?

I listen to my mother. I change into dry, clean clothes, bathe away the mud and blood, and sit curled in a blanket, rocking myself in the rocker before the fire.

✢ October 8

Uncertainty lies in the fruit bowl
on the table of my incentive.
Ginsberg can sing sunflower sutras,
reflect on mescaline images,
Walt Whitman,
Ralph Waldo,
Thoreau
can be dis-or-bedient

Who cares? Do I?

Care. Care. Does anyone care?
if babies bloat in Asia
from malnutrition, disease.

Or care, if in Colorado
the Rockies are guinea pigs
for nuclear reactors?

Or care, if international affairs
become domestic and scour sinks,
vacuum filth?

Or care, if in New York,
Wall Street crashes,
dragging to depths of
Depression the men
of depression?

Who cares? Do I care?
I have no incentive to worry.
I have no inclination to move.
I have only the repercussions
of my fall. I can only sit
and pick from my cheek
yesterday's scab

✠ October 9

An unwelcome event greeted me this morning. It lay over the ground in a cover of wet, white. I panicked when I woke up and saw the trees covered in snow. Winter is here, and I've so much to do—gather wood, finish chinking, haul in supplies. No sun shone today. Birds sang only in disapproving belief.

It was a long hard day working outside in the snow. By noon I had felled, hauled, buzzed up, and stacked underneath the cabin a cord of wood. Snow pellets and flakes bombarded me as I sawed. I shook my fist at the sky and yelled in disbelief, "Hey, you're not supposed to do this for another month." The winds that whipped snow about the mountains did not refrain.

Finished chinking today. One month chinked to hell, only because one month of chinking is hell. I am finished with this monotonous task. I very warily scaled the ladder to accomplish what I did and now feel alive and healthy because my labors have secured me a tight home.

All this hard work is a detour from the road my mind can take into fits of insanity—"insanity," for lack of a better term to call those periods of frightful melancholy I experience with more frequency now since the advance of winter. I think if I spend more time exerting my body and less time exercising my mind, I will be better off.

✝ **October 10**

Ann, the ex-nun turned lesbian, said to me one crisp night in Minnesota when we were swinging on a rope, hanging from a huge elm tree on a bluff overlooking the Mississippi River, "Yvonne, you are a privileged daughter." She smiled and put her arm around me.

"What do you mean?" I questioned and would have been hurt had she not smiled and put her arm around me.

"You have, at eighteen, what women all over the world strive for. You have money and a mind, meaning the sum total is power," she explained.

A turbulent wind causes an ocean-like commotion in the trees. In violent stage whispers, branches speak of winter's approach. It is so fierce a wind that the stovepipe creaks; the wind blows down the pipe and fans the flame; an occasional gust clatters the windowpane. I caulk and weatherstrip the door to barricade myself from the chilly infringement of the wind.

And the wind
she is fury
she is rippin'
and ragin'
she is a bender
of the tamaracks, slender.

The wind
she is blowin'
ashes and soot
birds,
in her gray
territory.

What constitutes being alone? Is alone the same as lonely?
I do not feel lonely tonight sitting beside the fire; the roof
over my head protects me from the storm outside.

✛ October 11

Eve of the cabin warming. Doubtful if anyone will show,
as rain and snow have made the roads treacherous. Ann and
her two friends drive from Montana to come to the cabin
warming. Ann's dog, Vogel, got into a porcupine, and I had
to run him down to the neighbor's to have the quills removed
from his snout.

Haven't done much work today. I took a short sketch trip,
but the cold drove me back inside. I set up a still life of deer
bones and pine cones, still wet after retrieving them from outside. The drawing begins with a good start, but proceeded
rapidly downhill as the day's light dwindled. It was not dark
enough to justify lighting a lamp, but too dark to draw without straining my eyes. I don't think winter light and drawing
are going to mesh well in the days to come.

✛ October 12

Ironic that the message of his death should be carried up
the muddy mountain road by the same neighbors who had
come to help me celebrate my new life in this cabin.

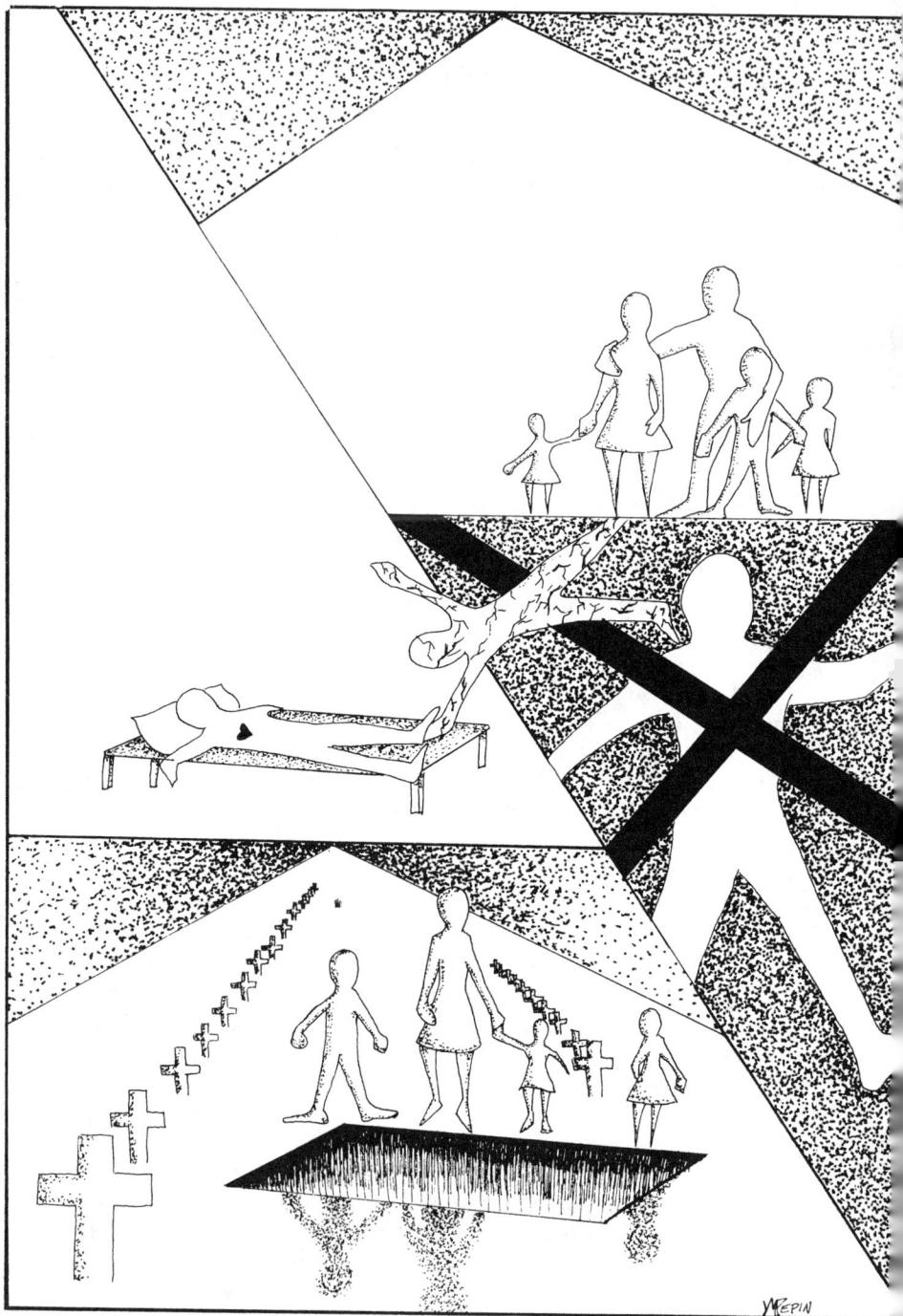

I hadn't expected anyone to come today, because the roads had become an impassable mess due to a sky that couldn't decide between dropping snow or rain. But they came on foot, the neighbors and friends who have taken to me since I moved up here. Almost everyone came whom I had invited. I served a lot of hot apple cider and cookies.

The end of the day was letting itself be declared by turning gray. I was cleaning up after the last of the guests when a motor rumble announced more people. Will Johnson had driven up his family and Jake Gray's family in a two-ton, four-wheel-drive flatbed. When they were all inside, with the mud of their travels clinging to shoe soles, I could tell by some artificial lightness contrasted with the solemnity of their faces that something was wrong.

"Before we stay," said Will, "I have something to tell you."

I knew then, as I had known with my father, with my mother, through the premonitions in my belly. Before Will could say anything further, I answered the statement he was sent to make as I answered the priest sent to tell me five years ago.

"She died, didn't she?" I told the priest as he brushed the snow off his collar after closing the weathered-oak door of my Minnesota home.

"Yes," came the reply. "It was God's will," concluded the priest.

"He died, didn't he," I said to Will today in my new home, a log cabin in Oregon.

"Yes," came his reply.

I didn't pursue an interrogation into the hows and whys of his death. I just stared out the window and let my emotions rest in the rain, the full rushing creek, the darkening forest shapes. I let hot tears brim, but bit down hard on my back molars to squelch my wet emotion. Grandpa was dead. This Frenchman, who would kiss me on both cheeks, who took me fishing, who taught me how to play cribbage, who was the only relative I felt was a relative to me after my mother died, was now dead.

Not wanting Grandpa's death to spoil the festivity of the occasion the neighbors had traveled to celebrate, I turned from the window and said, "Would you like some hot apple cider?"

After they had all gone, I sat alone in the maple rocker, in the light of one kerosene lamp, and wrote to the nurse who had been there when he died. I wanted to know the how and whys of his death. Grandpa had been the only relative who believed and supported me in what I am doing.

✢ October 13

I decided not to do any work around the cabin today. Instead I had a funeral for Grandpa. I walked the land and looked and felt he was with me.

I hiked to the top of the mountain, a place of vision. I sat up there and thought how much I had hated it all, my life of these past years.

I had felt cheated being an orphan, felt disregarded by and resentful of the surrogate system set up to replace my parents—the trust officer, legal guardians, probate judge, and lawyers who all had a say over my life. I was Yvonne Mary Pepin, ward of Ramsey County, under legal jurisdiction of this board of men. I had hated being beat up by my foster father, powerless in his strong hold as I was helpless to change the circumstances of my life. Those years of living a life I didn't want to live were like trying to survive in a lightless pit. I could not see beyond the black. Those years had made me dark, cynical, bitter.

But something happened to me today as I sat on the mountain. I started to let the dark go, relinquish the past to the mountain winds. I felt new life and fresh air finger freedom through my hair into my heart. I walked down the mountain thinking how I didn't want to carry all the hate and bitterness anymore, how it is all too heavy, and that a heart, like a back-back, should only be filled with light essentials if it is toted over the distances.

It was dusk when I was making the last bend on the ponderosa tree-lined road up to the cabin. I stopped under a stand of them, dwarfed beneath their branches. The trees reminded me of the ones Grandpa and I had planted in the swamp in Minnesota. Those spruce trees were never going to

branch out this tall, but they still represented what was alive between us and would grow. When I looked up at the ponderosas, I yelled, "Grandfather," into the darkening day. The trees swayed back and forth, sounding like an ocean. Then there was stillness, and I knew Grandpa was with me.

✝ October 16

"Snow, snow, blow away, come again some other day." I was singing this to the mountain this afternoon as the winds sent silent snow-filled flurries swirling around the area where I was sawing. Gusts would rip through the naked tamarack and cause the trees to collect clots of white. When I would stop the saw between falls, there was a silence new to me, filled with the ominous beauty of winter.

This snow excites me as much as it scares me. It puts a new color into my life—white desolation—and intensifies my reality of trying to winter it alone up here.

I suck on chunks of ice colored with bark and dried mushroom impressions. I improvise songs about my life up here as I fell and buck up the trees; not in the actual process of felling and bucking do I sing, but afterwards when I rest, between sucks of icicles. I keep repeating one stanza, which goes like this.

In my piney woods home
I am all alone.
To know my piney woods home
is to not be alone
in my piney woods home.

✛ October 17

I am a miniature version of a logger today. My boots crunch and snap twigs that pierce the bracing air. I swing an axe in one hand and carry the chain saw with the other. Around my neck hangs a block and tackle with forty feet of half-inch nylon rope I use to pull down leaners.

My boots, size three, are probably one-third the size of men loggers'; so are my plaid shirt and britches. I also bet they don't wear cotton underpanties. In the afternoon I get brave and decide to fell dead trees larger than I've ever attempted to buzz down before. Yes, I am hesitant, and yes, I'm afraid, and yes, the thought of having a tree butt knock my head off doesn't appeal to me. Yes, I think it is wise to wait until someone is around to help me in case I hurt myself. But I don't recall anyone's ever saying I was wise, so I commence cutting.

I flash back on everything Dale has taught me about felling. I circle the base of each tree, trying to determine through its lean and branch mass the path it will fall. I execute first the upper, then lower cuts, proceed to knock out the wedge, then begin my back cut on a 40-foot dry pine. There's a creak, a crack, then snapping bark. I do not even turn off the saw and begin to run out of the way, the opposite way of the fall. The tree goes crashing down in the path I've predetermined, but hangs up on some branches of a neighboring tree. Cautiously, I give the butt, still resting on the stump, Kung Fu kicks, hoping to dislodge the leaner. Kicking does not work, so I tie a rope around the butt and pull, pull hard, until the tree dislodges to the ground with a dramatic display of needles and branches.

154

✛ October 19

From the window nearest the stove, I watch a magpie perched in a tamarack across the way; its long tail feathers send a linear shadow on the branches.

Felling trees is becoming as easy as eating cupcakes, with my rapidly growing felling experience. Fell, limbed, and hauled half a dozen trees today with no problems except for one leaner that in spite of all my extended efforts would not budge from where it still lies, wedged in neighboring treetops.

So vain I am that I wish someone would walk up the road and see me felling, see me among all my logging equipment— chain saw, gas can, oil can, grease gun, socket wrench, two rolls of rope, axe, and pulleys. I am proud of myself: the exertions of my labor, to this evening, have pulled in over four cords of wood.

Outside tonight the moon is full and sending silver shadows over the ground. It is a little cloudy; an occasional shroud surrounds the moon's shining face, causing a white mist to halo.

✛ October 20

I've been working so hard this past week getting in my winter wood; that is all I've been doing. I begin to question my sanity, since the majority of my time is spent in the company of Tamarack and a chain saw. Hard work that leaves me exhausted and filthy takes the romantic notions out of this rugged individualist ideal.

I'm getting so secure behind the saw that I don't even need to use a wedge anymore. After my cuts, which gain in accuracy with each fall, I wait for the crack and run before the tree topples, taking branches of its neighbors on the way down before it crashes in a swirl of needles. It's a powerful feeling when the fall is right. I think I begin to see why loggers log—and why they don't.

What it seems to be about is self-reliance and keeping a stiff upper lip through all those times of "I can't do it," only to find that if I really get behind something, I can usually pull it off. I am learning to become my one-and-only—my own mechanic, mother, maid, logger, etc., etc.—everyone to myself out of necessity.

Tonight as I write in a yellow circle of light, my fingers shake from the saw vibrations. It is difficult to control the pen, and my ears won't stop ringing. Tamarack is getting on my nerves because he won't leave me alone, just sits on my lap, on my journal, and bats the pen, meowing. I think he is spooked by the inky night that spits pellets of snow against the windowpane.

✝ October 21

Felled eight trees today, and the saw had its first baptism of blood. In the casualness that comes with familiarity, casualness that causes carelessness, a laxness that sends fingers, toes, legs scrambling into the forest undergrowth, I cut my leg with the chain saw.

I was pulling out from buzzing up a log and grazed my leg a few inches above my knee. I felt no pain at first. I cut the saw, sat on a wet log and looked into the tear the teeth had made in my jeans. Blood was beginning to ooze into the torn denim fibers, and I wondered if I was going to bleed to death. I pulled my kerchief from my pocket and tied a tourniquet above the wound. Upon further examination, I discovered the slice was only superficial, exposing barely enough meat to draw flies. Still the cut hurt, and there was grease and oil in it from the saw teeth. I'd nonetheless shocked myself into the realization of how easy it is to bleed to death in these woods, and I sat on the log a little while longer to pull myself back together.

✝ October 23

The heavy snow falling all day subdued any incentive I had to write, paint, or even think. I felt like a lump, sluggish. I just sat in the rocker for long periods, falling with the snow.

Tonight, despite my muffled, muddled state, I lit the Coleman and went upstairs to draw. First I tried a rendition of a log with some small mushrooms growing from it. I began in washes of ochre, raw umber, burnt sienna, and defined the

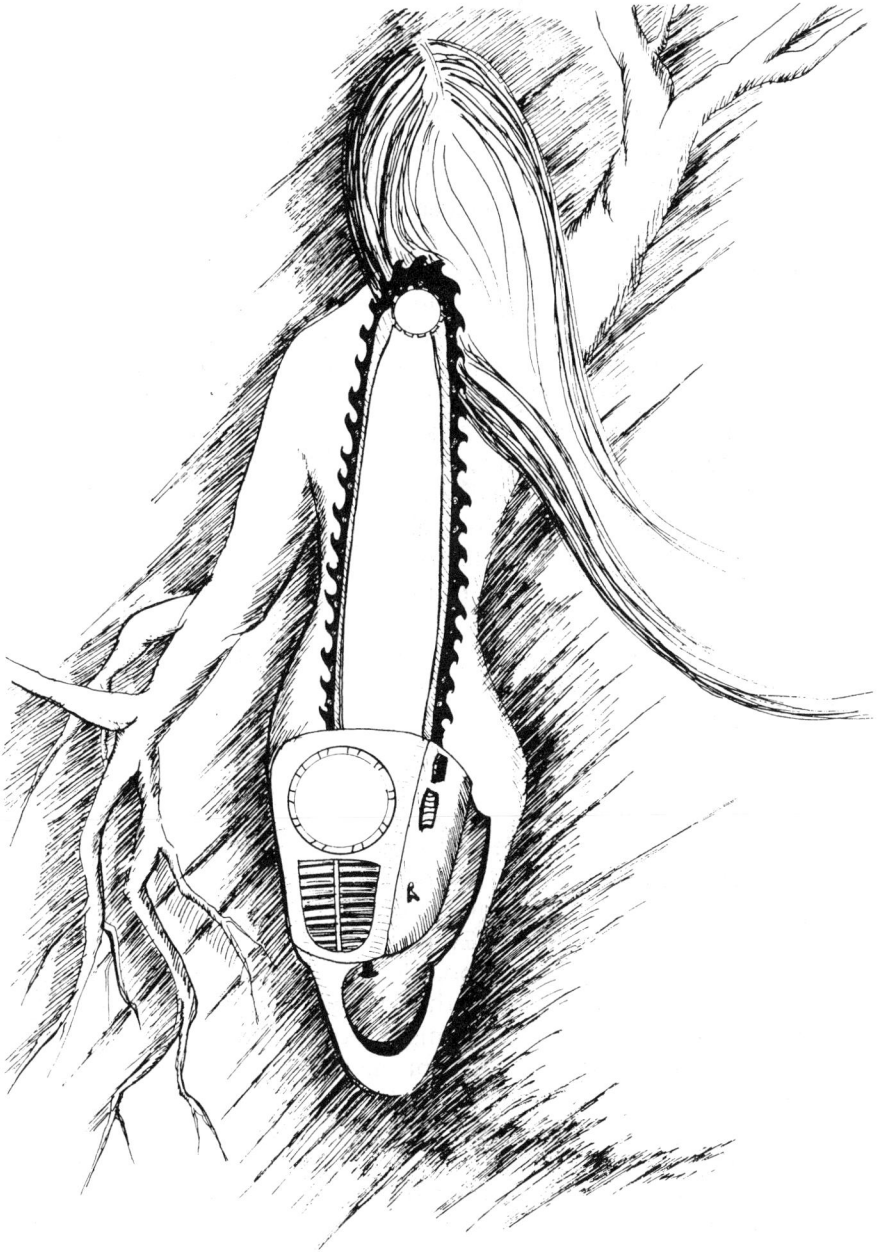

drawing with pen lines. I felt feeble, uninspired, drawing this riff. It was when I began to ponder my inabilities to express myself, entertain myself, that the sky I was looking at through the window provided me with the creative mood. Black pine silhouettes jetted into the moonlit sky. I began a pen and ink drawing. That drawing took no effort to create; it drew itself.

Around 2:00 A.M. the moon had arched across the sky to a degree where I could no longer rely on its position as a design element in my drawing. I quit and left the loft strewn with papers, pens, brushes, books, wads of this and that—one mess I enjoy making and leaving. Downstairs, I washed my brushes out and discovered that it took as much water as it does to wash my face. This meant an extra trip to haul water. I saw more clearly that it is going to be complicated to incorporate both my creative and survival sides into this mountain life.

Yesterday I felt the urge to draw in the morning, but could not because of work outside that needed to be done. When I was through and inside the cabin, the light was too poor to see by. In the city, I would have just flicked on a switch for instant light, giving little if any attention to whose or what resources I was consuming. In the mountains, I do not light a lamp unless it is very dark; I try to utilize all daylight to my advantage, because if I don't, then I consume kerosene, which means I will have to carry more up here on my back.

✝ October 24

The day decided to let up on its release of blowing snow, and gray skies gave way to partial sunshine. Now, with the fall of night, the sky's motions are drastically transformed into fierce, biting winds. Even though there are six inches of insulation under the floorboards, cold air swells up from the cracks. The wind is so brisk that it blew the cooler top off the porch. Truly, it is a scary night outside—definitely not an evening to read Poe if one is prone to a runaway imagination and insomnia.

I built insulated boxes for apples and canned goods this morning, then putzed around the cabin being tidy. Arranged some fruit in a silver bowl on the table and thought it looked so beautiful that I did a watercolor of it. It was 2:00 in the

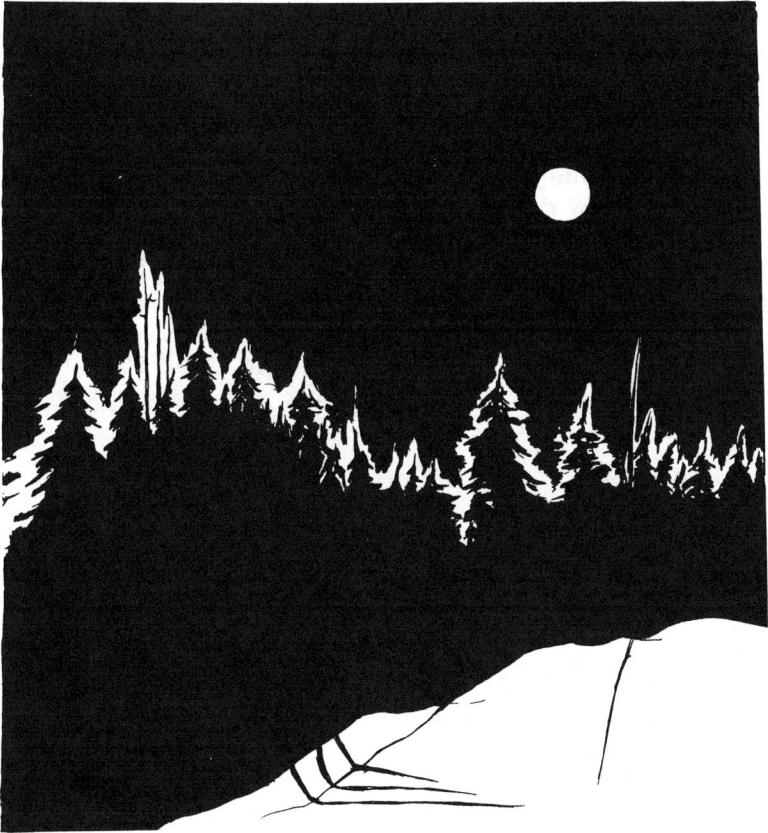

afternoon before I got outside to work on my wood supply.

The trees I fell proved to be exceptionally hard work. I sweated up my clothes and removed layers of them in the forest. Even though it was Friday, I sang "Groovy Tuesday" while I shouldered out sections of logs from the woods to the road, where I threw them in the tank's bed. I had chained her up, so could barely drive on the flat snowy ground.

✝ October 27

It falls hard and heavy, two inches in the last hour. Inside the cabin are smells of drying rose hips and bean stew. In celebration of the winter I have broken open a bottle of wine from my stash of two bottles. It is a dry burgundy and warms the insides.

"To you, dear winter!" I stand before the window and raise my silver chalice to the flurry outside. This snow is a concrete barrier between my life in this cabin and any people who exist around me for miles.

The past few days have found me engrossed in my creative endeavors. I've written three short stories, plus doing several watercolors. I find short-story writing enjoyable, but, like drawing a picture, I have to quit writing in order to step back and gain perspective on what I've done. It is easy for me to do this in drawing, but when writing I'm afraid to pause for fear of forgetting the flow of thought.

✢ October 30

In town today I buy a used portable typewriter at a garage sale for $19. I have to carry it back over the mountain in the evening, the other arm cradling a sack of groceries, a full pack of clean laundry, books, and other supplies strapped to my back.

I go to Pete's Barber Shop in the afternoon to get my hair trimmed. In the old-fashioned shop there are two other customers waiting to get cut.

"Pete, how much for a trim?" I say.

"I don't work on women," he replies, a little hesitant.

"Why not?" I ask.

"I don't know why not, Gawd Damnit! I just don't work on women."

"Well, why not, Gawd Damnit?" I mock, leaning against the empty barber chair.

"Because I won't! You're embarrassin' me." He turns to the other men customers and says, "Hey, come on, fellas, give me a·hand. Give her a good reason why I don't work on women." The men just laugh.

I don't give them a chance to reply by quickly interjecting my threat, "Pete, I'll report you to the ERA."

"What's that?" asks Pete, now red-faced and flustered.

"The Equal Rights Amendment, meaning it's illegal to not cut my hair," I answer.

"You would really do that?" He turns from the gray head he has been clipping to look at me. Pete has just been busted for dealing dope and is scared of getting in more trouble. "You bet I will," I say, "if you don't cut my hair." "Oh, Gawd Damnit, I'll cut your hair," he says, "but after hours with the shades pulled."

"Pete, cut it during hours like you would a regular customer," I enforce.

"Oh, all right, Gawd Damnit, you're after the next guy."

Later, I am in Dr. Pruitt's examining room. When I make eye contact with him, his eyes roll back beneath quivering eyelids. He is sounding technical and efficient, like a medical dictionary. I snicker behind his back, the scene seems so amusing. I have sought his advice as to why my period has not been for several months.

He is a stern young medical dictionary, diagramming on the white paper covering the examination table with a ball point pen the cause of my inovulation. I cannot decipher his fast, spidery scrawl or make any meaning of the pictures. After many minutes of textbook jargon I cannot understand, I ask him to simply say what is wrong with me. Dr. Pruitt says my inovulation can be from three causes: 1) ovary failure, leading to infertility; 2) pregnancy; 3) Ahserman's Syndrome: no lining to respond to estrogen.

Pregnancy is ruled out after a test is made, so it's one of the other two, unless there is a remote chance of a tumor on my pituitary gland. He says many tests have to be made to prove my problem. I say, "Thank you for your help. I'll be back when I have good medical insurance." At least Dr. Pruitt has a different opinion of my problem than the other doctor I saw in May, who diagnosed my inovulation as an aftereffect of jumping into the cold creek water.

Driving home, I am depressed until I see Dr. Pruitt's codfish face loom up into my memory. I begin laughing and slapping my knee as I see him draw a tiny uterus and fallopian tubes on the white paper-covered examination table.

When I am packing over the mountain at dusk, loaded down and tired from the day, I have pangs of wanting a loving person to be at the end of the journey. There will only be the dark and cold cabin that I must kindle warmth in, alone.

I strain every muscle to move through the snow over slippery hillsides. The anticipation of night and the strenuous work dissolves any loneliness I am feeling. At the end of my haul, Tamarack is waiting on the porch, crying to be let in and fed —or crying because I have returned.

✝ November 1, 1975

It is queer, this living alone, this life which is rarely shared with others. I often wonder how this solitude will affect my personality, my tolerance for people, once it is decided that I should return to civilization.

I am becoming a young spinster, living in my self-exacting environment. Everything, generally speaking, is done when and how I want it, with no regard to the desires of another. The only influence of direction on my days comes from the weather. I wake, bed, eat, and work when I will it. My life is strictly self-defined now, and I know it will lead to a harsh transition when I decide to move back to the city.

Will my spinsterhood allow me to grow to appreciate others after such an absence of human heartbeat, or will it sour me to the ways of others because the patterns I have created for myself hold me to my ways? I wonder if re-entry will close the openness I have developed in my spirit.

As quickly as I've begun to taste the joys of women, I close the cover on the delights and move into reclusion.

I think back to April, two days before I am to leave on the

trip to Pine Valley. I have come to a meeting sponsored by the Lesbian Resource Center. It is a coming-out group to support "peeping lesbians." We are all women in a room with dark blue carpeting and some bright orange beanbag chairs. We are all women who have come to this meeting because of a common understanding or question. Are we lesbian? We are all lesbians.

Two women, both younger than I, of high school age, lean against the wall. One of them looks as if she is on a bum trip. I wonder if they are young lovers. Another woman is squat, with orange hair and a patch over her recently operated-on eye. There are a couple of hefty women and one stereotypical dyke type, who wears a blue satin vest and a painted tie around her neck and has a head of short hair. Two nurses sit in observance on the sidelines, looking as if they have come out of a fashion picture magazine. When the question goes around the group, "Are you a lesbian?" every woman but these two answers in the affirmative.

The leader of the group says we all can ask a question. There is a long silence. No one moves to speak about what they have come to talk about. I break the hesitation by asking why the women here chose to become lesbians. The silence now is even more uncomfortable. I feel my face flush red in the wait. Finally, the butchy woman with the painted tie goes into a monologue about how, when she was little, her mother would never let her go outside to shoot a bow and arrow with the boys and instead made her stay inside and taught her to sew. I have used up my question, even though it was not answered. I feel a definite lack of commitment to own up to the statement "I am a lesbian" from everyone in the group.

Two hours before that coming-out meeting, A. and I sit in the Maryland Cafe drinking coffee. She tells me about her infatuation with Mary Pruitt, my boss, how she just wants to hold Pruitt. I tell A. how I've felt the same thing towards Pruitt. This leads into discussing our infatuations over other women in the college.

We have broken down a barrier between us, a barrier that is not diminished in the straight world, where it is strictly taboo to talk about one's desire for one of the same sex. A.

and I do not mention our relationships with the women we live with. We hem-haw around that we have very communicative relationships with our roommates. A. and I part that evening closer to the truths of our lives than before. I leave, wondering if she is wondering about me as much as I wonder about her. I do not even tell her I am going to the Lesbian Resource Center directly after our conversation.

The next day we meet again and reveal our sexuality to each other. This honesty between us sparks a quick lover relationship. A. introduces me to the gay bar life, since she is twelve years older than I and has lived in the circle I am just coming to know.

The day before I am to leave for Pine Valley, a group of women from college take me out for a drink. In the candle-light of the Holiday Inn Bar, we joke about each other's breasts. Cindy, the short redhead, says to me, "One morning you came into art class, and your nipples did salutes through your shirt. God, did that turn me on." It is odd for me to hear a woman say this about me—even odder that I do not feel uncomfortable about it.

Ellie is a lesbian whom Allan introduces me to. He wants me to get to know other lesbians, he says, so an informal gathering takes place at The Town House, which leads to Ellie's and my becoming friends. Ellie invites me over to her house a few days before I leave for Pine Valley. She lives in an entire house of lesbians. In her kitchen she hugs me good-bye. She is soft and pliable in my arms. I wish then our times together have been more.

Ann, the ex-nun, calls me a "privileged daughter" the night we drink Scotch and swing on the rope overlooking the Mississippi. She comes to bid me farewell the day I am packing to leave Minnesota. She says she has just bought a new hat. "Real dykish," she says. The word "dykish" is as uncertain to me then as is this life I have now made for myself in the mountains.

In my last few days of city life, I really start to come out. I begin to feel comfortable with my sexuality, begin to feel support from other women and joy because of our sharing. Now I've exiled myself to seclusion, but I cannot forget the taste of my freedom to be a woman with other women. I have just begun to open the door a crack; inside, though, I know, stronger than ever before, that I am a lesbian.

✝ November 2

Sitting before the fire this evening, I watch the coals glow red. I make no effort to kindle the flames, merely gaze into the dying embers.

It has happened. I have become stagnant to the point of no incentive to produce all those drawings I dreamed about in the busy summer months. Winter and aloneness have sucked me dry of inspiration. I make a discovery before the dying fire tonight. I've decided I've proven to myself that I am strong enough to live the life of a mountain recluse, that I can survive relying on myself, that I have learned to be a friend to myself, but I cannot sustain myself in a happy emotional state through the winter months. I need movement. I need a change. I decide to return to school for winter quarter. My decision excites me. Suddenly my life takes on fresh meaning.

This morning, while I gathered rose hips, I found myself actually missing the spice of city life. I want the music of stereos, the sound of conversations that provoke the mind into new dimensions. I want to draw the perspective on concrete city blocks.

People are what I seem to want in my life now. I am bursting with energies to flow in that direction. I am excited about getting into the lesbian movement, the women's movement, politics, the world of art and theater. I want to spend days in the forest of libraries. It will all seem like a new adventure after this absence. I think my time away from people has helped me grow stronger in myself. I think I can see more clearly what it is I need and don't need from people. Hopefully, through this understanding of myself, I will know when I am playing games and when to stop playing in order to communicate honestly, from the heart.

Nature in her raw but unrefined forms has taught me a truth no other person has. The words of people have never been as honest as the single arch of an elm tree. People have never given me answers like ice flows breaking up and floating

165

down a river during spring thaw. I have learned to find, through nature, my self in a way that I will never find through people.

+ November 6

I was hiking over the mountain by 7:00 A.M. this morning. Going-to-town day, with the anticipation of mail, a hot shower, and food somebody else had cooked. Also, Dorothy had asked me last week to join her at the Mormon Relief Society meeting. I was going to learn how to embroider. I was excited, in a sense, because it would give me an opportunity to talk with other women. Since moving here, most of my conversations have been only with men, about valve jobs, chain saws, building and so forth.

By meeting time I had put the day's errands inside my pack, which bulged full. I had shiny clean hair and wore all clean clothes—Levis and a flannel shirt.

Inside the carpeted, fluorescent-lit utility room of the Mormon Church, I felt out of place with women who were genuinely warm to me and wore dresses and things that would tear on the slightest snag of a branch.

One of the younger women was assigned to teach me to embroider. Her hands were the lily-whites they use in dish soap commercials. My hands, by comparison, looked like the scouring pad she would use on the crustiest fry pan. My fist fissures were imbedded with chain saw grime; there were calluses on my fingers that struggled to hold the hairlike needle and constantly shook because of the chain saw motor instilled in my nerves.

I had made a nice start on the dish towel I was embroidering, but it just seemed like there were other things I should be doing. I said my good-byes, politely, and left. It was time to get home anyway; in two hours it would be dark.

I walked over the mountain at dusk with a full pack, forty pounds of my life in layers: clean clothes, food, building materials, and the cream of luxuries—four volumes by Virginia Woolf.

The eggs fell out of the pack about a mile from the cabin. I couldn't salvage any of them and just watched egg yolk

mingle with snow. I was angry because that meant I wouldn't have any eggs to eat until I went out in another week. It put me in a crabby way to return to the cold cabin in the dark.

✢ November 7

One can say a leaf is green, the candy is red, the dog is black, your eye is blue, a frog is green, but one cannot claim fire is a single hue.

Today, I rise after an eleven-hour sleep and fill my knapsack with cakes of dried watercolors, paper towels, two plastic containers of water, paper, pen, and a lunch. I scale the southerly slope in search of an interesting subject. My eye detects many interesting compositions, but to render them is beyond my abilities. I do not cry, "Sour grapes," but remove my shirt on the snow-pocked hillside and lean against a lot in the sun. I spend half an hour trying to capture the fallen-pine hillsides, the standing-pine hillsides. I paint them loosely in washes. I catch a grasshopper in the jar I've emptied of my pen nibs to take home for further study.

✢ November 8

Living alone like this, I become aware of the different phases I go through. I become sensitive to the spirit that moves me to draw and write. Sometimes for days she leaves me alone; then other days she will not let me stop long enough to rest.

I wash my hair in the icy creek tonight. It's the biggest pizz-zazz I've had all day.

✢ November 10

It was a snowy Minnesota night last February that found Jean and me at a Boogie above the Green Grass Co-op. Ellie had invited us to a dance, a mixture of straights and gays. We drove in Jean's jeep. Ellie liked to be called a dyke.

On entering the huge hardwood-floor hall, Ellie went directly over to a group of women, and they all hugged her. All the women had short hair. Jean and I stood in the corner. We

168

both had long hair. Ellie and the other women, about seven of them, all started to dance together in a cirlce on the floor. They were a circle by themselves among all the other dancers. I asked Jean to dance, but she said she didn't feel like it.

A friend of mine from college, John, was there and asked me to dance, so I accepted. We twirled around, but I was always conscious of moving with a man and wanting to be included instead in the group of women. I broke away from John and began to dance alone over the dance floor in the direction of the other women. I gave Ellie the eye in hopes she would give me an eye of inclusion and I would be invited to dance with the other women. Ellie simply nodded, and I kept dancing, feeling estranged. John found another woman. I went off to the sidelines to find Jean, but she had left with two preppies from the University to go outside and smoke a joint in the Jeep.

Knowing Jean had left the room, I felt freer and gyrated all over the floor, my hair streaming, my shirt flopping after its tails had become untucked from my jeans. I moved my way over to the group of women in a gallant display of my dancing coordinations. They were dressed in vests, straight-legged Levis, and plaid shirts. How come they all had their hair cut short? Was this to be a Lesbian?

The closer I danced towards the dykes, the more I smiled at them. I wanted them to know that I love women too. I wanted to be recognized by them, to yell out, "I live with a woman and we make love. Most of the time on the waterbed, sometimes by candlelight in the bath tub, occasionally by the kitchen sink." Of course, I did not yell. I wanted the dykes to see it on my face, which they wouldn't even look at. They turned their cheeks to my smiles. What, I wondered, can I do to gain acceptance? Defeated, I went to find Jean.

The next morning, staring up at the ceiling, I connected my rejection by the dykes with my long hair. "It is my hair," I thought, "my long, fine brown hair." I was discriminated against by those dykes because of my long hair, which did not make the statement their short hair made. But I was not trying to make a statement.

This memory of the dance happened upon me this afternoon while I burned brush. The wind sent cinders and flame airborne, which threatened to lick me. I did not want my hair burned, so I tucked it up under a stocking cap. In the baggy wool sweater and jeans I wore, and my hiking boots with red laces, I thought I made those dykes look like marshmallows. Maybe now they would ask me to dance with them?

As long as I am discussing my sexuality, a question of great concern now is, What to tell Jon? How to tell him about my desire for women? How do I let him know that I can still love him and love women, though my sexual preference is inclined towards women? How do I keep from alienating Jon with my honesty? Maybe this is enough reason to remain a celibate mountain recluse.

It's snowing hard outside tonight. The brush pile still burns, an orange glowing mound warming the snowfall.

✚ November 11

Dale came today and finished the porch steps. They are immaculate—solid and sturdy like the rest of the cabin. The treads are a tamarack log split in two. The stringers, which the treads are spiked onto, are also tamarack poles. My only regret about the stairs is that I had nothing to do with their completion.

Dale had brought Sophie, and she and I took a picnic lunch up onto the south hills where the sun shone. She was impish, looking like Piglet in her long wool sweater and scarf. We ate lunch, and she asked me a million questions and hugged me often. She is so intelligent now at four; I wonder what she will be at fourteen, forty. I stretched out in the sun, and she lay beside me, then crawled on top of me, peering into my face.

"Dion," she said, for this is what she calls me, "are you ever going to have babies?" and she put her little hand on the humps of my breasts underneath my sweater.

"Maybe," I replied, "but not for a long, long time."

"Well, why don't you get a father and have a baby?" she continued.

"Because, Sophie, right now I like to be by myself."

We went back hand in hand down the slopes, over the creek. She helped me put the floor on the outhouse.

It is snowing thick flakes this evening. My throat is sore, raw; it hurts even to swallow rose hip tea. I have an ear infection also. Feverish, cold, tired, I just want to be lying in the waterbed under warm covers, being cuddled. All I have now, though, is myself, the winds which force themselves with a hollow sound down the stovepipe, and a kerosene lamp, lit for company.

✛ November 12

It is 6:00 P.M., and I have blown out the lamp to sleep. Yesterday's sore throat has progressed downward into my chest, and I feel an acute case of bronchitis coming on. It feels as though my throat and lungs have been scoured harsh, making breathing and swallowing painful. I've tried to keep my outdoor activities to a minimum so as not to breathe the cold air. I've drunk three pots of rose hip tea to try and wash out this sickness, but still my condition worsens. I feel terrible, wish someone were around to help me take care of myself. Being ill and alone leaves me feeling empty and helpless.

Two hours after I've doused my lamp, I awaken in terrible pain; I can hardly swallow, and my breathing is so shallow I'm afraid to fall asleep. I try to call Tamarack, but no words will pass from my throat. The fever makes me shiver. Every time I cough, I lurch involuntarily, eyes water, and oh, the pain.

Outside, the wind is strong; the blowing snow against the wall logs sounds like pin pricks. I barely have the energy to lift another log onto the fire and shake with chill until I can get it together to get up and put the log on the coals.

To be nineteen, alone, very sick, with snow-carrying winds that blow through this remote mountain saddle, is definitely a heart-rending sequel for "As the World Turns."

✛ November 13

My temperature is 103 degrees. It is an effort to move my pen on paper, but I must write in my journal; it is my only companion besides Tamarack, but he offers me no words. I am too weak to lift the maul to split wood and just get wet wood chunks lying on the porch to throw them on the coals, which simmer them into warmth. I know I need to get to a doctor, but I can't walk over the mountain to my truck.

Later: I keep waking in the night, tossing in sweat and pain. The daytime is no different. I am caught in a limbo of sleep and consciousness. I lie in my cocoon of a bed, watching the day fuse into night, a succession of values. My cough is sharp like a knife and brings up thick, blood-laced mucous. I am afraid of dying, alone, but later accept the consequences of this all-consuming fever that burns away any clear thoughts.

I try to cope, remain positive, but my physical condition rules out an optimistic frame of mind. I try to paint and preserve positive images of myself, strong images, and hold them in my thoughts. I must paint positive images of myself or burn with this fever.

I try to find some message in this solitude sickness. Throughout the night I lie awake with the pain of a skewer turning inside my chest. I am like a small child and want to be held and rubbed gently and reassured that I will be all right. I remember how my mother used to take care of me, and I try to do it for myself. This is the lesson realized—that I have given myself the power to be tender with myself, be my own source of nurturance, my own mother.

✝ November 14

I am cuddled up in the rocker, the same rocker my mother once rocked me in when I was a child with pneumonia. She held me in a blanket, and I watched the flames dance in the fireplace. Everything then was cushioned because of my fever. Today, I have no mother but that which I find in myself. I hold myself and stare into the dead ashes. I wonder how I can manage to get dressed and summon up the strength to split wood; there is none left to burn, and inside the cabin it is cold.

While I am thinking that I'm just going to freeze up here, I hear a motor sound. I look out the window, and a blue pickup with chains on is coming up the road.

"Oh, Miller, damnit." I do not want him to see me in this wasted condition. I'm still upset with him and his midnight adventures a few nights ago, when he came up after I had gone to bed to "Take me out to dinner," he said.

Today, Frank says he has been concerned about me and came to check on me. He splits a pile of wood and stacks it on the porch. Then he drives me over to my truck. I drive to town, go to the doctor's, get a prescription for antibiotics, and go home, back to bed.

+ November 15

If I'm better in a few days, I'm going to take a trip to Eugene and check out a college to attend this winter.

+ November 18

I put two plaid shirts, two pairs of jeans, one wool sweater, my extra boots, clean underwear, my journal and sketch book into my pack. The roads were packed with snow and were icy. I drove over the McKenzie River pass as dark fell. I arrived in Eugene around 8:00 P.M. and am staying at Pam and Tom's house, two people who own land near me in Pine Valley, but live in Eugene in the winter.

+ November 19

Yee-hawww! I've found women in them thar city blocks! By accident I stumble into a small restaurant for lunch—Gertrude's, a lesbian-owned business. Inside, there is an array of different types of women, all having lunch. They have short hair, long hair, dykish looking and not, some wearing skirts, some hiking boots like me. The waitress sits down with me to take my order. When I tell her I am new in town and ask if there is a women's center, she fills me in. There is to be a panel discussion by Del Martin tonight at the University of Oregon. I also learn that the college I'm thinking of enrolling in, Lane Community College, has a women's center.

I spent the afternoon checking out Lane, the women's studies department, the art department. I like the campus, the people. I am going to enroll there in January. I can't believe that I am committing myself to make this change.

173

Everything is falling into place. It will be interesting to see what this coastal city life can give me. This fresh start again will be another test of my independence, my ability to survive in the wilds of people instead of the calm forest.

At 7:00 P.M., I attend the panel discussion given by Del Martin. She is an older woman, butchy looking, with her silver hair brushed straight back. I recognize her as the woman who sat at the table across from me at lunch today. The auditorium is full of women; I can distinguish many lesbians by feel. As usual I am the youngest in the crowd. They must think I'm a kid of about twelve years old. I think it will be hard for me to be accepted by the women's and lesbian movement because of my youth. I try not to be conscious of my age, because it makes me feel inadequate and immature.

Del Martin begins her talk. She gives a short history of lesbians. I learn that the gay activists' movement began in the 1950s, supported largely by the Daughters of Bilitis, a San Francisco-founded organization of lesbians. The first lesbian periodical was *The Ladder.* I am educated in the struggles and oppression that gay men and women have had to undergo in the past twenty-five years. Compared to the social conditions then, my coming out now should be as smooth as cream cheese.

I write Jon tonight to tell him I am not going to return to Minnesota for the winter as he had hoped. I can already feel his sorrow. I am selfish. I put my happiness before his.

✦ **November 20**

I spent the morning seeking out various women's organizations in Eugene. This town is loaded with women and women-operated resources. There is a women owned and operated press called Jack Rabbit Press; Mountain Movers, a feminist literature center; and Mother Kalia's, a woman's book store. At Mother Kalia's I bought *Women, Our Bodies, Ourselves, Lesbian Nation, Lesbian Connection,* and *Country Women.* The young woman behind the counter and I had a warm conversation about our sexuality. I felt charged with women's affirmations today. I didn't feel like I'm weird or queer because I choose to live independently of a man and love women.

I ate a supper sandwich at Gertrude's this evening and was well into my third cup of coffee when one woman came and sat down to talk with me. Turned out she is from Minnesota also. Soon the table had other women clustered around it, and I seemed to be the center of conversation. They wanted to know where I'm from, what I'm doing here. They seemed to like me, especially after I told them I've built a log cabin in the mountains and live there alone. They invited me to a lesbian party tomorrow night.

✝ November 21

The lesbian party did not live up to my expectations; nor, generally, does anything. The party was held inside an old gray house with women's symbols painted on the front porch. When I entered, I was greeted by a short, squat woman with a band-aid on her cheek. She introduced herself and accepted me warmly, then showed me around to the other women in the house.

Two women were sitting on a couch giving each other foot massages; two other women were involved in a conversation; and a lone woman with thick glasses sat in a corner stapling papers together. There were more women in the kitchen eating from a table top covered with bowls of munchies. During my introductions, I felt they warmed to me. All the women had very short hair, and next to them I felt out of place, about as comfortable as a rose in a snow field. Even after others entered the party, I remained the only woman with long hair. I felt the other women wondering about me.

Movies were shown of a celebration of women at Coyote Creek, Oregon, a hundred-acre parcel of land owned by women who let only women live there. On a white sheet taped across the wall, images of women making love in meadows, swimming in a pond, painting each other's bodies, dancing, playing music flashed by. Most of the women were naked, laughing—jubilant to the awakening of their lives. Their breasts were all sizes and bounced under the sun. Not since the eighth grade Phys-Ed have I seen so many breasts in a grouping.

The Coyote Creek film was returned to its canister, and

the projectionist put on a reel of the 1968 Democratic Convention, which featured Alan Ginsberg holding a sunflower. After a few minutes of that, the women retreated into the kitchen, where there was dope, food and drink. Not knowing anyone there, I remained in the living room, disinterested in the film and waiting for a cordial "Come into the kitchen and join us" invitation, which never was verbalized. So I remained in the living room, doing what I do best, observing. The house was full of women in short hair. Some had whiskers on their faces. They wore clothes like gypsies and had names like Pinecone, Witchhazel, Space, Crow, Thyme.

Soon I tired of observing and got my coat and boots to leave, which meant going through the kitchen to retrieve them. I had to cut through a grand assemblage of women engaged in intimacies with other women or dipping into the avocado dip. Some eyed me, others brushed me off, no one said "Hi" or any word that would induce me to want to stay, so I left.

I went to my truck and slept for three hours, awakening at 4:00 A.M. and heading out of Eugene for the ocean. My eyes felt like hot sand; I coughed and felt cold and damp. I was out of Eugene and traveling down Highway 126 west. The moon hung outside, a reflection in my rearview.

It's 7:30 A.M. I sit on sand dunes, desolate and windswept. Whitecaps roll in the distance and crest above the ocean's surface. I feel fine—like a free woman.

✝ November 22

A seagull cries, dropping tear-shaped shit into the sea. Sandpipers, always an inch ahead of incoming surf, gather morsels by the shore. Surging white and green waters break against calm sands, the lacy white of the surf frothing brown with its contact of beach.

My feet are wet; an incoming wave caught me by surprise. I have rolled out my sleeping bag and try to sleep in my bedchamber of cold sand under a gray sky ceiling. The air smells salty and heavy with moisture. This ocean air is not like the cutting edge that the mountain winds blow but more like a thick meal in my nostrils. I can't sleep because I wonder too much if the tide will come in and take me out to sea while I slumber. I get up, hungry, and walk to the truck. I. sing "Good-bye America" and kick up piles of sea foam; they blow skelter in the wind. Having had only six hours' sleep in the past two nights, I am so tired that I shake.

I drive on to Agate Beach, eat, then try to get some rest. I lie on the beach for almost an hour, then get up and explore the ocean-surfaced floor. I squat above delicate bird prints on the beach sand and sketch them while I sing.

Couples walk by on the beach. A child and a mother walk by, hand in hand. The scene makes me feel lonely. I do not feel connected to anyone. No one on this earth knows where I am now. I could die, and no one would know it. It is an ominous feeling to be so alone, without destination, without home, without anyone to know or care where I am.

✛ November 23

Spend the night on a muddy turn-off just outside Nebo. I wake up inside the truck to sounds incomprehensible. Discover after fully waking up that it is pouring out. I hurry and pull my pants on. I do not want to get stuck in the mud on a deserted roadside in the middle of the night.

It is 3:45 A.M. when I am taking curvy coastal roads, simmering in pouring rain. At 5:00 A.M. I am the only woman, except for the waitress, in a grungy little coffee shop, drinking coffee. Three cups of coffee, a face wash, and I'm back on the road.

I watch the sun rise over a deserted beach, to reveal the endless ocean horizon. The wind outside is so powerful it rocks the truck cab. I have my breakfast of corn chips, broccoli, cheese, and fig newtons. When I go outside to pee, the wind pushes my pee stream perpendicular to my crotch. I have just defied Newton's law of gravity.

At 7:15 A.M. there is enough light in the sky to see the whitecaps rushing into the shore. I go for a walk. The winds are strong and cold, and I have to stand spread-legged while zipping up my raincoat, lest I be blown out to sea with the gulls. Damn, it's good to feel the energy in winds that push out stale spirit from my soul and implant it with ocean force.

I like to feel the belt of wind in my face, the pull and out-stream of wind gushing through my hair, the kind of wind that makes footing unstable. The sea, like a familiar friend, is known but not totally understood. Waves wash up onto the shore to greet me. I stand and honor my old friend, in silent reverence for her spirit, the power and mysteriousness of her salty powers.

The ocean is my first love. We have a simple and complex affair, as simple as her surface waters, as complex as a biopsy of a 110-foot deep slice of this aquatic biology. My love for the ocean is precisely why I've chosen to live in the mountains. What is that saying? "Absence makes the heart grow fonder"? Well, my adaptation is: once you get to know a lover, she (he) becomes less of a lover and more a way of life, as familiar as a favorite pair of socks, comfortable and taken for granted.

I am a solitary figure walking on the beach this early morning. The sands are a natural broach, inlaid with the finest colored sea jewels and polished by the shove and suck of waves. Broken sand dollars are scattered on the mocha brown sands. Jellyfish are shimmering here and there, their amber transparencies like cellophane motioning in the wind. It is high tide, and I know so much more lies deep down below the eyes of the ocean surface.

On a rocky point perpendicular to the stretch of sand I've explored, I stand and watch the incoming waves swirl. Intent on the waves' action, contemplating each curl of foam, outburst of white surf, I do not realize until too late that a wave has scaled a rock in wet layers of salt lace, and it cascades over me. I am veiled in the salty sea. Saturated, I walk back down the sand stretch, feeling stupid at being caught off guard by a wave.

A gull feather lies transparent on the sands, a gift of retreating waves. My pants, sopping wet, hang below my hips. Ocean foam is blowing across the lacquered sands like amoebas scattering on the slide of a microscope. A husky dog runs up and sniffs my leg, then runs over to a boulder and lifts his leg, sending a yellow string of urine into the wind. Back at the truck, I change clothes and continue north on 101.

A few miles down the road I stop at a deserted park—
Oswald is its name, and it is owned by the State. A 0.6-mile
trail through the woods of gigantic redwoods, lush foliage and
ferns, moss and ivy captures the variance of greens in the area.
A sign posted near a woodpile reads: "Wood for sale. 50 cents
for 2 cubic feet." I think back to my home, where I burn for
slash what they sell for fuel here. The law of supply and de-
mand connotes the reality of the pocketbooks shelling out.
The path opens up to Necarney Creek, and I walk beside the
rush of fresh water falling into the sea. The trail holds speci-
mens of human life—bottle caps, a used condom, gum wrap-
pers; signs of the ignorance of this animal lie strewn on the
forest floor.

Necarney Creek leads to a cove with an enormous pile of
driftwood logs on the beach. Sun rays that shine on the bends
of the cliffs fall on the soggy redwood, which evaporates cold
moisture in the hot beams. There is mist in the entire cove except for this patch of bright, steaming redwood. For the first
time I notice seagulls have bright yellow beaks. I walk back
to the truck, pick up litter, and stow it in my pockets; it is
wet sop, slop. I sing improvisations.

Drive ten miles or more until a sign says "Cannon Beach."
Here I turn off to discover another pocket of this coastal life.
The tourist trade has pockmarked the ocean front with concrete motels poured onto the beach sands and signs proclaiming, Buy this . . . Eat that . . . Sleep here . . . It costs only . . .

I eat a hunk of Swiss cheese and an apple on a rock facing
the ocean. Gulls swarm overhead. I walk down the beach to
be left alone, but they follow me. They are used to the human
hand holding food. I yell at them to go home and leave me
alone, thinking my shouts will scare them away. My own
voice yelling at wind and birds makes me think that this
beach is the gulls' home, and I am the intruder. I should be
the one to go home.

At 10:45 P.M., I am gritty-eyed from driving but elated for
no apparent reason, trying to glide the truck through rain and
fog. I sing "Bobby Magee" with Janis Joplin on the tape deck,
both windshield wipers slappin' time. I teach myself to avoid
crashing over cliffs while driving fifteen miles over the sug-
gested speed on hairpin curves, changing tapes with one hand

and steering the wheel with my elbow. I learn how not to and how to properly spit out the window in the wind. I just keep driving until I can't anymore.

✝ November 27

It is Thanksgiving Day. A fresh powdery snow covers the mountains. I sit before the fire after morning chores, warming my moccasin-covered feet and feeling thankful (no religious significance) for all that I have, all that I am. There has been no place that has felt finer to me in the past week than my little log cabin in the woods.

I felt like an entry in the Daytona 500 as I drove my last several hundred miles home yesterday. I shifted down and accelerated around curves and punched the gas hard on straight roads swiping through flat grass lands. I rolled into Pine Valley early last evening. There was a pile of mail in my P.O. box.

I walked up to my cabin in the dusk with a full pack on my back, a burlap gunnysack of groceries in my hand. It felt good to feel familiar muscle strain after so many days of hibernation in a truck cab. I heard the silence in falling snow, an occasional drawn-out whisper of pine, an owl hooting in a ponderosa snag, and the constant swush of Dean Creek. I took off my pack above the hill that leads down to Ann's cabin. There was smoke coming out of the stovepipe, and yellow light made bright the usually dark square windowpanes.

I gave my familiar "Hooody," and Ann opened the door to reveal a scene anything but charming. Inside the cabin there were three ragged-looking males cleaning a pound of dope: my brother, my cousin Phillip, who has come from Puerto Rico with his friend I just call "Worm." We are all going to have a happy Thanksgiving together. I asked Ann if she would like to spend the night at my cabin.

I told Ann about my sexuality last night. She seemed more accepting than I ever imagined she could be. It has taken me a year and a half to get my nerve up to this degree of honesty. Telling Mark will be a different story.

I fondled all my letters, then began to open them in degrees of priority. The one from Jon confirmed the date he will arrive here to spend Christmas with me. I opened another envelope with no return address on it. Inside there was a card with a picture on it of a cool green landscape with a small flowing creek, and inscribed above the picture the words: "We arrive in this world alone, we depart alone; this time called life was meant to share." Inside the card face, written in Jean's tight hand: "The reflection of two women in the fresh mountain stream reveals their secret, absorbing sun's rays, touching nakedness, caressing in love. I remember . . . I still love you, Yvonne. Jean."

I am elated with the card. I've wished for these words every day. Now that they are here I can't help wondering if they are true words. I do not know what to make of them or of Jean's intentions. I am feeling hard towards Jean.

All day today I spent with my family, partaking in the gluttonous feast of Thanksgiving. Mark said, "Dinner's ready. Come get it." And the dead, brown, baked bird was ripped and knifed apart, then layed to rest on gold-leafed china plates. The turkey's inner cavity was aborted of stuffing. They poured brown gravy over potatoes, meat, and vegetables. I ate a salad and was chastised for my preference. Four faces shone in the grease of dead meat.

After supper the "men" all remained seated. They groaned in their overindulgence and chewed tobacco, spitting the sludge into coffee cans. They cracked jokes about "layin' chicks, teats and balls and suckers and cocks." For once, instead of spouting reproach of their talk, I remained quiet. I knew their ignorance would prevent them from hearing anything.

Ann and I were putting away the leftovers. I was wrapping up the turkey neck in tinfoil for Tamarack and said to Ann, "Have you ever read *Inside the Bell Jar*?"

"No, why?" she asked.

"Well, there's this section in there," I said, still intently staring at the meat I was wrapping in foil, "where Esther is shown by her college lover, Buddy, his penis."

At the word "penis," Phillip, the Worm, and Mark pulled from their talk to the conversation I was having with Ann.

"When she saw his crotch," I continued, "all she could think of was turkey necks."

Ann and I both looked at the turkey neck I had in my outstretched hand, smirked, then broke out laughing.

When I packed up to walk home a few hours later, Phillip and the Worm had laid down their *Playboys* and were thumbing through *Ms.*

✝ November 29

Feminism isn't a new awakening for me. I have always been independent in my nature, but the feminist consciousness and support of other feminists are new to me.

So many days up here I've felt alone, like the only woman in the world struggling to learn to use tools and find alternatives to do traditionally "male" work. It's been a struggle to compete with men because I must always work twice as hard in comparison. I achieve sometimes only half the results that a man could because my body is smaller, my muscles not as large as men's. It takes me twice as long to fell a tree, to build, because I am learning to use tools and my capabilities I've never touched upon before.

My momentary outburst is a fragment of the anger I feel from having been subjected to the male ego. I asked Mark to come up and help me lift a five-hundred-pound barrel of kerosene up onto a stump I was going to use as a cradle. He came up bringing the Worm for reinforcement. The stump had to be leveled first, and when I was carrying down the chain saw and axe, Mark tried to take them away from me.

"Here, want me to do it?" he said, reaching for the tools I withdrew from his grasp.

I began to level the stump. Mark said, "May I make a suggestion?"

"Yeah," I said, listened to what he had to say, then began to serrate and chop out the wood chunks in my own fashion.

"Oh, here, let me do that," Mark said, again trying to grab the tools from me.

I said, "No thanks," and chopped away even harder then. I was tired and fed up with having to always prove my competency in the eyes of those who think I am incompetent. I was crabby all day.

In the afternoon I tried to ski the anger out of my system. I glided very fast, unhesitantly taking steep hills, ignoring the consequences of a fall. I was almost fearless in my anger. Macho Woman sails over the meadows, through powdery snow until . . . a cluster of pine trees appeared in my pathway. Cross country skis do not afford control to downhill racers.

I could not avoid crashing into the pine trees. In a poof of snow and flash of pine needles, I was down and aching because I had hit my butt on a rock. When I'd recovered from the shock and pain, I rubbed my ass and said, "Damn!" loudly. The word echoed in the valley a repercussion of my collision.

I was not far from Ann's cabin. She heard me and yelled, "Cookies," an opportunity I could not pass up. I refastened my skis to my feet and resumed my downhill racer attitude, able this time to stop short of the creek before an icy plunge. At Ann's I ate my belly full of hot, fresh chocolate chip cookies. Instead of skiing home back up the mountain, I moved like stiff sludge up the slopes.

✢ November 30

Since June, the gray remnant of a wasps' nest, an ornament of ash, has hung from the soft green needles of the tamarack. July and August came; the nest adhered itself to the branch despite heavy rains and winds. September and October turned the tamarack needles to gold, and still the wasps' nest hung. November's cold winds and snows stripped the tamarack of its golden attire, and the tree stood naked, a stark, intricate black skeleton.

It is, today, a few hours short of December. I skied by in the day's dusk to spy the hornets' nest fallen and lying like a piece of soot on the snow. This old friend, which has brought my line of vision upward every day, now lies limp and pliable like soggy onionskin paper. I touched it, picked it up. It was so delicate it crumbled in my hand. It was silent, the fallen wasps' nest. The pine above roared in heavy mountain winds, and I skied on, knowing in spring the nest will absorb back into the earth's skin.

I skied and walked about four miles today. In the morning the sky was dropping snow all about; by afternoon it let fall rain and mist. The snow got sticky and packed down, making skiing slow and strenuous. I built up a heavy sweat and removed my shirt.

It was about 3:00 P.M. when the sky told me it would be dark soon, so I made my way for home. It was very windy, and the trees let loose their blankets of snow. A fine mist blew strong through the air. I stopped skiing, put my shirt back on, and stood in observance of my conifer friends. I began to feel lonely, knowing the distance this winter is putting between me and other life. Then these dark green cone-bearing companions were absorbed into my bones, as if by osmosis. I felt their spirit. I could hear their musings. The trees gave me strength and raised my spirits. I began to sing. Song and pine was something the doctors never prescribed for me when I was devoured by depression.

My song was about being alone and discovering a strong self. I sang myself into a strong place and remembered why I came here—to be alone, to learn to hold myself and find the strength it takes to build strength.

I examined the trees on the way home, which ones need to be thinned, which are diseased. I am learning to read the forest like a book. I live in a library of trees.

Inside the cabin, having rekindled the fire and sitting beside it warming my feet and drinking tea, I forget about being lonely and watch fat snowflakes collect on fir branches.

✝ December 1, 1975

Spent the entire morning finishing the first article I've ever written. Trying to organize my thoughts was like trying to saddle up a herd of mad hornets. I've addressed an envelope to *Country Women* to stuff the article in and mail to the address inscribed. I will anxiously await my first rejection notice.

It rained all day and pushed two or more feet of snow back into the dark earth. I put a log full of hibernating ants on the fire today, not knowing the ants were inside. They came to life in the flame, scurried all over the burning log and were burned.

✛ December 2

When in the presence of others, I am not as strong as when I am alone. When I am in company, my tenacity slackens. I know if I fall among friends, they generally will help me back up. When I am alone, I do not let myself fall, as rescue operations are too time-consuming and there is no one to help diffuse the pain after my descent.

I took a long walk in the night. It was black as the space between the teeth of a cheetah. I didn't use a flashlight. The sky was like glittered licorice. As usual the forest was a foliage silhouette. I kept a tight rein on my imagination so the creatures of my perverse thoughts would stay hidden in corners of my mind, the corners I do not seek out for fear of finding what lurks in the dark spaces of my thoughts.

Walking back, though, my imagination broke loose with horrible and frightening images running in packs. Tree stumps turned into bears, and behind every tree waited the butchering men. Up on the porch, night animals cowered, hunched in wait for their prey, ready to slash me with claw-studded paws. When I opened the door, I fell over a body still warm and wet in a pool of blood. When I lit the lamp, the murderer stood in the corner with his knife ready for his next victim. His eyes were wild and his teeth bared. When I sat down before the fire and removed my shirt, a voice from the loft called my name; then there was shrewd laughing. But I was afraid of none of it. To be afraid would mean to be afraid of myself. I am not afraid of myself anymore. I put my imagination to bed.

✛ December 3

One would assume—and, since I am naïve, my assumptions generally bring with them a great degree of naïveté—that being so young, living alone, leading a secluded life would be simple. Though I may be a simpleton in my ability to comprehend, I am not apt to make my life simple; the aim is simplicity, but not my manner of achieving it. It seems I put myself through a maze of complexity before I find that simple way to the end.

I packed a trunk full of clothes today and sledded it down the mountain to my truck. I am preparing already to move to Eugene.

When I walked through the Doc's meadow, I stopped and had a psychic chat with the barren apple tree. Over a month ago, the tree stood leafy green and hung red with apples. Now, it looks sad, a skeleton, with only dry yellow leaves that crackle in the wind.

We talked about changes, the apple tree and I. We have both budded green in the spring, with anticipation of the ripening effects of summer. We have blossomed and borne fruit. We have stood up in all types of weather, circumstances dealt to us by the mountain that our only alternative was to put up with. We have had people pick from our fruits, steal

our fruit, treat our fruits badly. We have given freely of ourselves and been picked upon when we had no desire to be
picked at. The apple tree with its nobby branches now has
seen me through transformations and growth as I have seen
the apple tree through many changes.

✠ December 4

> ". . . there is more likelihood of sexual fulfillment with another
> woman as well, since all organisms best understand the basic
> equipment of another organism which most closely resembles
> themselves." —*Lesbian Nation*, p. 167

Like yesterday in observance of the apple tree, I look
today on the polymorphous nature of my sexuality. If homosexuality is hereditary, then through my parents and what I
know about their lives, I should be an adventurous, intelligent, thoughtful, yet a straight young woman. How did my
sexuality come about? Freud would probably say that my
condition is inherent due to the death of my mother, a rever-
sal of the Oedipus complex—that I am trying to find and ful-
fill motherly gratification in my desire for women now.

But even before the death of my mother, I found myself
gravitating to the female of the species. In sixth grade I fell
in love with Jodey Larsen. The day in Miss Stougard's class
when Jodey moved her desk away from mine I was crushed.
Even though her desk was only two behind me, I still went
home feeling dejected and locked myself into the bathroom
and cried myself sick. My mother had to phone up Jodey's
mother so Jodey would phone me up so I would come out of
the bathroom.

I wonder, though, if one doesn't fall in love with one of
the same sex at this stage in one's growth because of the
natural ways of human nature. I guess it is not until we
"grow up" and fathom the degrees of mores and taboos set
up by the system of patriarchal standards that gravitation
towards one's own sex is set before as a no, no, a perverse
turn in the established turn of events.

My first organized Amazonian tactics occurred in the
fourth grade when, in retaliation against the girl-shoving boys,
I organized a small band of girls who would attack any boy

pushing a girl from the playground equipment. I had acquired in the ranks of my little girl army thirty or more girls during the first week of school. We would line up on the playground during lunch recess, all thirty or more of us. I would march up and down the lines yelling, "Stand up straight," and orders on how we were to proceed with our attacks against the little boys. When we would see a boy bullying a girl on the playground, I would give orders, the girls would break ranks, run after the malicious boy or boys, tackle them, and unzip their pants. We sent more than one boy crying to the noon playground monitor.

The news of my army spread fast, and soon I had so many girls wanting to join that I had to hold interviews to see if they had what it took to be in my army. My flat-chested force became the terror of the playground. One day when we were about to apprehend a boy on charges of misconduct, we were surprised that the boys had banded together and met us with an army of equal number. A knee-skinning, hair-pulling confrontation ensued, a mass of squalling children that was broken up by several teachers and playground attendants. Word got to the officials. I was sent to the principal and assigned a three-week detention.

Jon will be here in less than three weeks to spend Christmas with me. I think about sending him *Loving Women* and underlining sections on clitoral stimulation.

✝ December 5

Loneliness pervades me like my breath, like the night that comes too early into this mountain saddle. By 4:00 P.M. there is no longer enough light inside the cabin to work by, and it is still too early to light a lamp.

This aloneness is omnipotent, something I can't shake or buffer myself from. It puts me up against myself, makes me face my demons and find reason to like myself even when I can find no reason. I have to learn to face myself and transcend these lonely feelings, to find creative and nourishing ways to explore these dark parts. This is winter now, winter of the heart. I understand why animals take to hibernation. It is only natural to turn in on myself.

189

✠ **December 6**

The simple facts of life I have taken for granted now strike me with great significance, like the texture and color of a carrot examined by lamplight. I chew each bite with renewed appreciation. It seems like a miracle to eat fresh food during this time of year when so much of life retreats beneath a frozen white shell.

Sitting down to write in this journal has been a ritual for me almost daily for the past nine months. When I haven't made an entry, I feel incomplete. What started out to be a school project has evolved into a mode of self-exploration, discovery, and has become my companion when there has been no one to be my friend.

At every sitting, though, I still feel inadequate to express myself. I am at loss for the precise word, the phrase that could articulate the feeling inside of me I am wrestling to express. I feel my use of language is uncultivated, inarticulate. My sentence structure is at basic first-grade level. I need some assistance. My ignorance and ill use of the language counteract my intentions.

If I haven't before—and I can't recall whether I have or not—I wish to record a fact discovered about the literature I've partaken in up here. Not the books separately that I've read, but on the way I must read in order to obtain healthy results in my emotional constitution. I must balance what I read. I must thumb pages that give equal amounts of elation and depression. Too much to one side of either subject would throw me into the illusions cast by that particular literature. If I read something flavored of melancholy, then I must also read something light. I give my consciousness something to chew on through the flip of a page, the flap of a book jacket.

I control my companions as easily as turning a page. If Kate Millet, Gertrude Stein, Hemingway, George Eliot, Tolstoy, Nicholson, V. Sackville West, Virginia Woolf—to mention just a few of my literary friends—were to say something to raise dissatisfaction in me, I merely close the book and go for a walk or engage in other activity until I have washed them out of my comprehension. Jill and Tolstoy make the word "stew" tasteful.

190

✛ December 7

Built a seat on the outhouse, finished shaking the roof, hand-sewed some curtains out of heavy golden upholstery material. I prefer the hammer and saw to the needle. At 4:30 P.M. shredded-coconut snow frosted the evening, and a yellow crescent moon hung in the sky.

I wrote something on the typewriter tonight called "December's Epic Emergence." It is not during but after a writing of this nature I wonder about my sanity. This side of me is not of the earth, lofty in the degrees of my mind's perversity. This expression of myself is removed from the me that runs naked over the mountainsides and sings with the land. Venting this darker side of myself I think lightens me up so I may appreciate my earth ties more. When I uncoil my mind, I divulge demons and exercise, exorcise them.

DECEMBER'S EPIC EMERGENCE

Tonight, she is an obsidian reflection cast to the windowpane of her doubt. Her constant companion, fire, has burnt low. Outside the cat meows for entrance. I lift the latch, then decide the feline is a stranger to me and foot it out the door. I imagine the cat a nun in habit, but disguised by whiskers and a tail, doing penance in this night chapel of dark silhouettes. The feline distraction has taken me from my friend the fire, which waits as my spirit does to be kindled. Throw some fuel on. Let it burn. Let fuel turn warmth into the cold night orbit.

The log is layed onto the death bed of coals and hisses not of warmth's desire but lulls motionless like a slug in the damp cellar basement. I think. What else is there to pass the time with but thought that takes you from thinking? I think that the solitude of this life teaches me not only to speak the worth of solitude but feel the hollowness of solitude's value in my heart that has learned to pulsate in the lone red blood flow.

I think of the many times I have been trampled underneath the feet of people who disregarded me like city pavement, a surface they use to propel themselves over. I think how I have taken on the characteristic of concrete. I think how I loved my mother as only a daughter can love a mother, as popcorn tastes better with butter. I think about my mother the way I refused to feel about my mother. I feel the softness that joined us, her smooth cheek and gentle eyes, which I did not want to touch me. Even in my childhood I held a front against anything nurturing that could broach the shell I retreated into, my dark and quiet pod.

I think of my mother now, what she has represented to me, how she now lies decaying beneath the surface of a Minnesota winter. Under the sod of a carefully manicured lawn. Happy Hills of the Ceased Heart Beats. The Cemetery of the Elite. The tombstones declaring she died, he died, when, where, how, and why. I see my mother's nostrils crammed hard with the decay of a life I once shared. She rests beside my father; side by side they partake in the delights of decomposition.

As there is no mother now to do the things for me mothers do, the things I did not like my mother to do for me, there is also no father in my life to dance with on Saturday nights, as in my childhood, with Lawrence Welk on the television and beer and pretzels in the background, while my mother looked on approvingly as only a mother can look when seeing the joy of daughter and father. I was one of the dancing apple dumplings during those festive family nights.

I think of the family I had and have not had. I think how dollars replaced love—though I could never love the dollar, the dollar could never replace the love of my parents. I think how, in the pretense of strength that would costume me with a cloak of invulnerability, I would not cry, not let on that, yes, I felt grief because of the family I no longer had.

I recall yesterday a magpie ripped the flesh of a road kill. It was raining, and the bird looked simple in its black and white markings. This image has stayed with me, not the death image, but that life may feed off, survive off death. That death may nourish.

✛ December 10

Someone could think by reading my journal that I have shut myself away in this cabin to mourn my losses of love.

On the contrary. My mourning is only the process of coming to gain strength through these losses. I do not bathe in the subtraction of love's force, but find other powers in its absence. I find powers in my darkness that love lets alone.

I try to conceive of myself, conceptualize all that I am. I do not know whether I have the insight or honest awareness to give me a truthful reflection of the life in and of my flesh. I try to see myself through my own reflection without the aid of another's opinionated face. Sometimes I feel so happy and confident living alone up here that I think, because of my elation, I am sick. Shouldn't I thrive on interactions with others? Shouldn't I desire companionship instead of shunning it? I continue to find contentment in my reclusivity, my simplicity. I enjoy seeing the change of seasons and myself.

✢ December 11

It's ludicrous how we can know so many people, yet know so few of the people we know.

✢ December 12

Snowed a couple of inches in the night. Again, winter pureness in my vision. Restless sleep last night. My dreams keep surfacing a recurring symbol: A gray rock formation towering over either the ocean or Lake Superior. I am always alone on the top or bottom of the rock, waiting for someone or something. Waves, incoming, barely keep from crashing over me.

I wish I had Jung's book of symbols or even a glance at Freud's *Interpretation of Dreams.*

Ground wheat berries and soybeans into flour (arm-bustin' work) this afternoon and baked a blueberry cake. I got the stove so hot I took off all my clothes. I thought it might strike someone as an odd occurrence to see me dancing around naked inside a log cabin, manipulating cast iron pans and stoking a fire when fresh snow lay all over outdoors.

I did some anatomy studies in the loft using my own anatomy. I squatted naked before the mirror and did a quick line sketch. The most articulate part is that point between my crotch. I like the sketch; it has spirit.

At 4:30 P.M. I went outside and split wood. A waning

slice of moon was pasted bright against the dull sky. I sang "Jingle Bells" to the rhythm of the maul in hopes of warding off my pre-Christmas depression.

I walked across the creek and up the mountainside to see the sky and if it held prospect of more snow for the night. I wore only jeans and a plaid shirt, no jacket, and felt the penetration of winter. Returning, I stopped at the creek for water and caught the moonshine, flecked golden, in the dusk-gray rippling creek.

✝ December 14

> The rich buy at Bloomingdale's
> candied apple fingernails
> lampshades laced with skin of whales.

194

leisure dollars earned through unmuscled time
red and green christmas ornaments shine
tis the season to be jolly
crammed of lust and spendthrift folly.

Buy your loved ones what you will
your pocketbook to open and spill
on trinkets for your void to fill.

It's christmas time in the city
ring-aling, cash registers sing,
its dollars green make this season pretty,

multi-hued lights that shine
garland and neon bring tinsel time

the birth of christ is acknowledged here
americans spend to christmas cheer

and admit their love for humans dear
with price tags of material leer

gold and knick-knacks of useless being
american dollars bring on meaning
infiltrating the market greedy.

And all the while at Bloomingdale's,
money spent on painted nails
knick-knacks to sit high on shelves,

runny noses in the ghetto cry
of the little boy, in barefeet
he's meant to die

of bellies bloated and vacant stares
from children in malnutrition's care

while dollars take on christmas cheer
masking the falseness, exposing the rich sneers.

material wealth this society shines
muffling those of harder times

while dollars spent at Bloomingdale's
could aid those with empty pails

merry christmas to all
and to all a good plight
you who buy at Bloomingdale's.

I was inspired to write this poem after reading an article in *Time* about the extravagances Americans spend money on at Christmas time. This poem holds somewhat true to my beliefs, but is hypocritical, since my material wealth puts me at a safe distance from poverty's plight. I sit high above the strife and abuse the majority of Americans must face daily. I have built myself a little fort away from the battles. I live in my shelter of logs, a barricade against the negative forces of the human being which heavy my heart. I can maybe shut out some of the sights of child abuse, malnutrition, disregard for the elderly, but the thoughts, the knowledge that these things exist whether I can see them or not, force through any wall I have set up in order not to see the elements of the human condition that heavy my heart. It is time for me to leave my princess-and-the-pea routine, the life of a privileged daughter, and go back into the wilds of human hearts to help where I can.

I brushed the snow from the truck this afternoon and drove into town to mail my Bloomingdale's poem to *Time*. At the county paved road, I had to crawl under the truck and pick the chain latches apart with a Phillips screwdriver. Fifteen minutes later, the latches, which had frozen the chains around the tires, were unclenched, but my hands were so cold I had very much difficulty unwrapping the chains from around the axle. I was wet and cold from lying on the dirty, snowy road, with grimy slush falling into my face from the truck's underneath. I wished I had someone to depend on who would help me. But after extreme effort, I triumphed over my discouragement. My accomplishment was simple, though it was great, because I have never before unlatched frozen chains from a tire on a sloppy country road.

196

It's the full moon
makes me wish to blame
you, whose doubt
has dismembered and maimed
love we once shared
that will never be the same

because your edge has
brought the pain
to cut this passion,
this love in vain.

I blame you not for our
love's duration, the pain
inflicted was a collaboration.

It's ceased.
It's over.
Our combined rot,

you are there
and I am not.

✝ December 15

Excitement was bounding in these mountains today. The
highlight occurred at approximately 11:00 A.M., stemming
from my decision of whether to use one or two squirts of bio-
degradable soap in the dishwater. Two—it was mused over
before confirmed—were used. The sheer ecstasy of longer-
lasting suds put me in an orbit of joy.

Now, as if I hadn't had enough elated intoxication for one
day, I was faced with another exhilarating decision: the
choice of whether to eat an apple green or red for lunch. In
my exuberant state I did not trust my senses to function
properly, as the adrenalin that still altered my perceptions
from my rendezvous with longer-lasting suds made it impos-
sible for me to come to any rational actions. In my ebullient
condition I chose green.

Now, most assuredly, if I wasn't young and strong, all this excitement would have taken a toll on my heart beat and finished me off before I could participate in a further extension of the joys life parades. Just as the action in my day was beginning to slacken, the fire needed stirring and a log had to be retrieved from the porch and placed on the embers, freshly stirred. It seems useless even to try to capture in words the emotion entailed in this experience, for words would only curtail the vitalness of my action.

The titillation of my day continued and would not slacken, like the pace of a dryer continually fed with quarters to keep up the momentum. I sat on the stovetop as I always sit on the stovetop and burnt my posterior in the place where a hole in my jeans exposed a bare fragment of my tender hind quarter to the hot charity of the heated cast iron. The administration of a cold compress to ease the blister down on the burn on my hinder was, it could be said, the confection that tops off the fare of a fine meal, or one more exhilarating experience.

It was 6:30 P.M. when I thought the agitation of the day's events would subside for a while and let me conduct my peaceful and orderly approach to my life. As I sat in my rocker, I felt worn from all the stimulation I'd encountered in my usually mundane day. But if there is one flake of snow falling from a winter sky, most assuredly there is at least another, then other flakes to fall. So it was; my storm of thrill did not end with the day, but continued on into the evening, when I had to decide whether or not to lace my coffee with milk.

✛ December 16

While I was taking a leak tonight, the moon above was almost full and cast a shadow in front of my compact, irrigating figure onto the snow-covered ground. A fast cloud grazed the lopsided white ball of moon and painted an orange halo onto a night canvas tinted in indigo with the exception of short scratches of starlight. Winds blew the heavy snow from the trees, and they swayed like winos in the night. Such are my companions.

Finished reading the International Women's Year conference report and bulletin this morning. I was impressed with the range of insight this year's conference directed to minority women. I was infuriated, though, by their lack of mention of and interest in advocating lesbians. I wrote a letter to ISIS, a nongovernmental agency of the I.W.Y., asking them to recognize lesbians as a minority and to give lesbians similar representation and support in future conferences.

Finished reading *The Death of Ivan Ilych* by Tolstoy. I was morbidly refreshed in memory of all the funerals I've attended. Towards noon, I grabbed a banana and headed for the south hill, where there was sunshine, and began reading *The First Circle* by A. Solzhenitsyn. In bed at night I read a cheery documentary, *The Plague and the Fire*, by James Leasor, a book about London in 1665 and 1666.

The moonlight reflections and cast shadows dazzle the night, and I think A. Beardsley could make a fine drawing from my surroundings.

✛ December 17

Through the time it took for me to make acquaintances in the city, I have made steadfast friends in Pine Valley.

Went to town this clear-cut morning. The sun was just beginning to crown golden the tops of scattered pine as I walked through the Doc's meadow. The sun was hoisting itself magnificently in red light; the frosted yarrow tops glimmered.

In town, took my weekly shower. Hmmmm. All because of bathing and a change into clean clothes, my self-image, self-esteem, rose 26 notches on the pegboard of my personal satisfaction. I bought X-mas presents, chatted with the townspeople, and showed them pictures of my cabin. I felt like a celebrity in a group of men; some of the same men who teased me in the spring ogled now and asked questions about how the cabin was built. A couple of the men saw the photos of me using the chain saw and looks of embarrassment crossed their faces. This is no exaggeration.

I drove to Butte City and at Sam Hampstead's house dropped off a loaf of bread I had baked in the Dutch oven. I told him if he wanted a slice of it to run the loaf through his mill.

Called Jon this afternoon. He will arrive here in five days. I anticipate his arrival and events that will ensue. I want him to be here, but I also want the option to be alone at my discretion. I hope for my sake he has learned something along the lines of clitoral stimulation, or he will get a strict tutoring when he arrives. Aside from his ignorance of the sensitiveness of my body, Jon is the finest man I've ever met.

The moonlight falls in silver squares through the windowpanes onto the floor tonight.

✛ December 18

To my mother:

in this rocker, rocking
before the fire now,
you held me
against pliable breasts
when I was a child.

200

i remember watching
flames ballet dance
in the grate, the feel
of your body stopping
my rambunctious moves.

now you have died,
five years ago
this march, and lie
in a box, and I have
learned to rock and still
my moves alone.

the rocker, since you left,
has made the rounds,
seen its share of scratches
and nicks.

used, the rocker has
been used. i use
the rocker, it rocks me
holding you.

The day is lucid blue, and I leave after breakfast to hike
the hills. It is cold. My feet rustle in dry snow. I find signs of
coyote, deer, elk—no tracks, just scat from the sources.

I climb up onto the red rocks and take my shirt off, shel-
tered from the wind in a cove where the sun falls on top of
me. I pull from my pack my copy of *The Sacred Pipe* and
begin to read, though my attention is more drawn to the valley's view that folds out in front of me. I feel compelled to
read, thinking that the words will teach me more than seeing
the sun shimmer on a spider web that whips almost unde-
tected in the breeze. From my vista I have the advantage of a
heightened perspective.

In the Indian "Crying for a vision" ritual, or "lamenting,"
men lament on the mountaintops. The "women also 'lament,'
. . . but they do not go up on a very high and lonely mountain. They go up on a hill in a valley, for they are women and
need protection." (*The Sacred Pipe*, p. 46) What would the

Indians think of me, I wonder, sitting above the valley so high, bare-breasted and snow lying all around me.

On "Preparing a Girl for Womanhood" (*The Sacred Pipe*, p. 116): "She should know, further, that each month when her period arrives she bears an influence with which she must be careful, for the presence of a woman in this condition may take away the power of a holy man." Even the most liberal of ancient people lived sexist myths.

✝ **December 19**

I discovered a xeroxed copy of "Betty Dodson Speaks on Masturbation, Erotic Art and Women's Liberation" among my collection of literary riff-raff. This find came just in time. Jon will be here in a few days. His four years of law school never versed him in the rights of a female's erotic zones. I will

have to tutor Jon, because I will not feign sexual fulfillment
for the gratification of someone's ego.

In high school when I was playing my role as "girl friend"
to a man ten years my senior, I used to fake orgasm because
if I didn't, my "boy friend" thought I didn't enjoy sex with
him. And I didn't, but I didn't want him to know it—something on my part about pumping the male ego in order to preserve my place as the submissive female. I gritted my teeth
over the years during insensitive sex with men. Some mornings I would come home from a rendezvous with a man and
fall into bed with Jean. I would cry because I thought I was
sick because I enjoyed sex more with her than the men I was
with. Those were unsure days, good days, days when I began
to define my needs by what I felt, not by what I was taught
I should feel.

Betty Dodson's exposé of a woman's control over her own

sexual fulfillment is very liberating; however, it is not exactly in my line of desire. Masturbation leaves me bored, and up here there is no place to plug in a vibrator.

I watched four deer feeding in the woods yesterday. I perched on my stump in the forest and noted down every move they made, their color and texture. I jotted down my notes on some paper, including the AUCCH, AUCCH, AUCCH cries they made upon discovering me.

To watch deer is one thing, to study them with careful vision is another, but to write of them when they are in my vision is to adulterate my vision and violate their privacy. When I returned to the cabin, I used the sketch I'd written on them to kindle the fire.

✝ December 20

You kiss me
in respect I close
my eyes at the dead.

I wished you
dental floss, a
cleansing action,

I awoke to your
wallowing tongue instead

warm wet slug

if only my nose were a foot
on the garden's face

one stomp would cease
the slimy trail
you trace over my path.

You thought I was
a frog pinned to
beeswax.

Dissecting, you called
it love and filleted me.

What did you see?
Something, that made
you leave and me splayed,

little lungs, a pulsating heart
no longer under cover,
exposed because of your
loving touch.

I was left painfully opened
you didn't bother with
formaldehyde to still
the rush of blood.

You left the room
and me, pinned, vulnerable
so I could watch you drop
an imitation smile

an additive, like vinegar
poured into what
I layed open to reveal.

✝ **December 22**

J. A. Madison writes, saying I'm more mature at nineteen
than she is at twenty-nine because I can accept the rejection
of a lover. I wonder if this is maturity—to accept and be
obedient to fate. I write J. A. Madison that she shouldn't
dwell on the loss of a lover but look for another love instead
of mourning what is dead.

Dorothy gave me some Christmas presents today: *The
Book of Mormons, A Marvelous Work and a Wonder,* and
Pearl of Great Price. She inscribed in the books that she is not
trying to push anything on me but to share something that's
very dear and important to her. I'm very happy with the

gifts, not because of the materialness of them, but the love behind the giving of the material.

I scanned the books tonight. They make an interesting set-off to *The Sirens of Titan*. The Mormons' doctrines and theories make good historical reading, but like all history, it is men who make history. I want a Josephina Smith to have had the visions Joseph Smith had. I want a Moronia, not a Moroni, to appear to Josephina Smith. In the account of Lehi, it was his four sons who bear the name of his adventures and not Sahiah, Lehi's wife. I want Sahiah's four daughters to bring the message.

The teachings of all religions I've encountered center around the patriarchal belief in God, the father, God, the son, the disciples, the prophets, the guru—all men. In my fourteen-year practice of the Catholic religion, eight of which were spent studying the catechism, the mention of women included the vile, wicked Eve, the Immaculate Conception herself, and Mary Magdalene. I want to read "herstory," that is, not written by men, recorded of men and their factual phallic bias.

✝ December 23

I can't concentrate long enough to read, can't keep my thoughts together enough to write or draw. There is a distracting force in the presence of my now infiltrated solitude. Jon rustles upstairs in bed, taking in some very deserved sleep. Is he the element fragmenting my thoughts?

There was a clump, clomp on the porch last night, commotion that startled me from my reading. When I opened the door, there was Jon with a pack on his back. He had walked over the mountain from where he left his van parked, following my tracks by moonlight.

Later I extended my little bed to include another, and when I climbed between the sheets, I found the other enthusiastic over me. Love-making was the smush of wet kisses, a fondling of the breasts, a parting of the lips, dry and not willing to receive penetration. It was for me unarousing sex. I felt intimacy, not stimulated. I know I will have to break out of my timid ways and show Jon the ways I want to be loved.

206

When he touches my breasts, I wish he had some to touch back.

✛ December 25

Merry Christmas, yuck! I search for words to relay the analogies of my negative feelings. I feel very wasted from yesterday's drinking bout. Alcohol and my metabolism don't boogie well in the mountains. I've been very allusive, grouchy, and just wanting to be left alone by Jon. I am finding it difficult to reciprocate his love. I rediscover that I would rather do a solo in my life style than a merger with another. Is it normal for one of nineteen years of age to want to live alone, to be so defined in the way I want to live?

I do not mean to be critical of Jon. He is understanding, perceptive, caring, gentle (for a man), all that I would want in a male lover—if I wanted a male lover, which I do and don't in the same thimble of thought.

This morning I did it, under the influence of my patience worn thin. I told Jon I wanted my clitoris stimulated. He did not even know where it was. I showed him, and he was very willing to learn. I am willing to be a teacher somewhat, but not a guinea pig. How must men learn about women if they have no teachers? In my growth and desires, I do not want to slow my own progress to tutor pupils. I gave Jon a copy of "Betty Dodson Speaks on Masturbation." I got dressed and went out to split wood. Jon stayed in bed and read. About half an hour later, he came outside, leaned over the porch railing, and yelled to me, "Woman, in all my years of college I've never been as enlightened as today!"

✛ December 27

I'm all packed for Eugene and will leave tomorrow. This is the last night these logs will shelter me for a while. I get a little chokey, knowing how much I will miss my home. I have cleaned the cabin, battened down the hatches, and have a pile of wood pre-split on the porch. In case I need to run back home from Eugene, I will be able to rekindle my life up here quickly.

207

I went to say good-byes this evening. At Dorothy's door, her eyes watered when we hugged each other. She said, "I don't know if you know it, but you're my other little girl up on the mountain." When I hugged the Parkers, it seemed they hugged me back tighter. There was a gloss of sadness in the eyes.

I got a letter from Jean. It seemed to me a pretentious flow of egotistical words. After I read it, I threw it into the fire, watched it ignite into flame, and followed the intense heat until it dwindled into gray ash. A realistic metaphor of our times together.

I am hesitant and excited. At this time tomorrow I will have reentered the mainstream of life. I'm in for some rapid changes and pulls in the current that will sweep me away from my mountain retreat. I am about to begin on another chapter of "Yvonne Grows Up." The future is waiting for me to prey, for me to become predator of the future.

✝   ✝   ✝